KANSAS TRAIN TALES

A Collection of Railroad History

by

Robert Collins

ISBN: 1-440499-16-0

Cover Illustration: The Santa Fe station in Marion, Kansas, has been restored and now houses the public library. The depot was also used by the Marion Belt & Chingawassa Springs railroad, a short-lived excursion line. The history of the MB&CS is just one of the stories contained in this book. *Author's photo.*

Published in the United States of America
January, 2009
Published by Create Space

TABLE OF CONTENTS

MAPS AND ILLUSTRATIONS

PUBLICATION CREDITS

This is where the articles in this collection have appeared, in chronological order:

"An Error In Timing," 1992 Jesse Perry Stratford Writing Contest, Second Place; also appeared in *All Aboard* (the Frisco Railroad Museum), Volume 8, Number 2, March-April 1993; also in *Territorial Magazine*, Volume 14, Number 2, March-April 1994.

"Trolley to the Oil Fields, " 2001 Jesse Perry Stratford Contest, Second Place.

"Otto P. Byers: Railroad Man," *Territorial*, Volume 22, Number 1, February-April 2002.

"The 'Samson of the Cimarron' Story," *Territorial*, Volume 22, Number 2, May-July 2002.

"The Saga of the Scott City Northern Railroad," *Territorial*, Volume 22, Number 3, August-October 2002.

"Sabotaged by Fate & Greed: The Transcontinental Chance of the U.P.E.D.," *Territorial*, Volume 22, Number 4, November-December 2002.

"'Another Terrible Massacre' and the Victoria Railroad Cemetery," *Wild West*, Volume 16, Number 5, February 2004.

"The Marion Belt & Chingawassa Springs: Kansas' First Excursion Railroad," *Territorial*, Volume 25, Number 3, August-October 2005.

"The St. Joseph & Topeka: Kansas' First Ghost Railroad," *Territorial*, Volume 26, Number 1, February-April 2006.

"Two Railroads, Two Towns, and One Rude Surprise," *Territorial*, Volume 26, Number 3, August-October 2006.

"A Railroad as a Pawn: The Story of the Dodge City, Montezuma & Trinidad Railroad," *Territorial*, Volume 26, Number 4, November-December 2006.

"The Salina Northern: The Last Kansas Railroad," *Territorial*, Volume 27, Number 2, May-July 2007.

"The Kansas Southwestern: Two Railroads, One Branch Line," *Territorial*, Volume 28, Number 1, February-April 2008.

INTRODUCTION

Welcome to this collection of railroad articles I've written over the years. Some of these pieces haven't been published in years, some have come out recently, and at least one has never been published. I hope you enjoy the material in this collection.

I must admit that aside from broadly speaking being about railroads, there's no single theme to these works. Two cover specific incidents, five are histories of companies, one is a biography, and one is about a line that was never built. I think what does tie them together is that they aren't about the more famous aspects of Kansas railroad history. They're about people, places, and lines that can get lost amid the material that deals with the major railroads that appears every year.

You won't find action shots of the Scott City Northern in the news-stand magazines. There's little chance of an in-depth, 300-page biography of O. P. Byers coming out from a big publisher, or even a small press publisher. The history of the St. Louis & San Francisco railroad's branch line to Halstead is a tiny part of the overall history of the SLSF (better known as the "Frisco").

Yet the subjects covered in this book are worth reading about. Understanding why the Scott City Northern still isn't in existence is understanding how railroads were built across Kansas. If you know the story behind the Victoria Railroad Cemetery you can better appreciate the struggle to lay track on the unsettled frontier. And you won't find a more stark contrast between railroading in the Nineteenth and Twentieth Centuries than in the history of the Cimarron River Bridge project.

You might wonder why I wrote about these particular subjects and not others. The answer to that question is the same for any writer. We write in a genre, or about a topic, because it resonates with us personally.

For some of the articles here, the personal connection is obvious. I like the Frisco, and I live in Andover, and that explains why I wrote the first and last pieces in the book. Working on **Ghost Railroads of**

Kansas, I came to be interested in short lines. I've also taken a great interest in the Kansas Pacific, so much so that I'm working on a second, more-detailed history as a future project. As for the rest, well, sometimes a subject clicks for me, and sometimes it doesn't.

These works are also a bit of personal history of me as well as being parts of Kansas railroad history. There's a gap between the first piece in this collection and the rest. Insert the four books I wrote from 1996 to 1999, and you should get a sense of my growth as an author. I think I've gotten better at my craft, better at researching, and more confident in expressing myself over the years. That doesn't mean that the first piece in this collection isn't as valid to me as the last. I'm not ashamed of my work back then. It's just that I'm doing more and doing it better now.

Naturally, this collection doesn't cover every article I've written since 1992. I left out at least one railroad article from this, largely because it's too similar to another work that is in this collection. I'd like to put several of my other historical articles together in a different collection. If you like the material here and want to read my general historical nonfiction, let me know the next time you see me at a signing or giving a talk.

Finally, I'd like to express my appreciation to the publications that accepted these works and put them out, and to all of you for your continued support of my efforts at writing.

Robert Collins
January, 2009

AN ERROR IN TIMING:
THE ANDOVER TRAIN ROBBERY

In 1898 the small town of Andover, near the western border of Butler County, had a brief fling with the "Wild West." A train robbery led to an eruption of gunfire in the then-tiny community. But there might not have been one shot fired, had two wanted criminals not chosen the wrong Saturday to commit their bold crime.

Andover was served by the St. Louis and San Francisco Railway. The St. Louis and San Francisco, or Frisco, had built through the area in 1880. The citizens of Bruno township had earlier voted for $18,000 in bonds for the railway. With the construction of that line, the town of Andover was platted and established.

Andover was a rural community during those days. The only businesses in town before the turn of the century were a general store, a blacksmith, a lumber yard, and a grain elevator. The one church holding services in its own building was the Methodist Church. Andover had a small depot, roughly 18' by 32', with an office, a waiting room, a freight and baggage room, and an outside privy. It was these last two, the church and the depot, that would play major parts in this drama.

Throughout the day of July 16, 1898, two men were grazing their horses in the area. The farmers who saw the men assumed that they were cowboys passing through. They hung around for most of the day, but kept apart from locals.

That July evening the church held an ice-cream social. The whole town was in attendance. The talk of the town would have been the end of the Spanish-American War, as the final attack on Santiago, Cuba, was under way. There would also have been speculation on the harvest some two months away, and gossip about friends and family members.

Among the more well-known attendees was Frisco Depot Agent S.B. McClaren. McClaren was helping make the ice cream, but he had no plans to stay the whole night. He would have to return to the depot around 9:45 PM. The daily express passenger train was scheduled to arrive in Andover at 9:55 PM.

McClaren left the social on time. He probably passed by the

blacksmith's, and may have seen two men tying up their horses. The men followed Agent McClaren into the depot, and one of them bought a ticket to Augusta, the next town along the line.

As McClaren was preparing for the train's arrival, the two men revealed their intentions. They drew large-caliber revolvers and ordered McClaren to hand over all his cash and checks. The agent gave them about $45.00 in cash and $50.00 in checks signed and made out to a local creamery. The men then ordered him to flag down the train.

The Frisco didn't have a name or number for this train. An 1886 schedule describes it only as an express passenger train, running daily, heading east out of Wichita, with a 9:55 PM Andover arrival. The train's consist was probably a 4-4-0 American-type locomotive, a baggage car, post office car with express area, and several heavyweight passenger cars. No one would have known why the train was stopping, but wouldn't have been concerned.

As soon as the train stopped one of the men leapt up to the locomotive's cab. He ordered the engineer and fireman out of the cab, and kept them in front of the engine with Agent McClaren. His confederate then entered the express car. There was only one man guarding the safe, an express messenger, and he was unarmed. The robber ordered him to open the safe. The robber took the $400 or $500 that was in the safe, and left the car. It looked like a quick crime and a clean getaway.

But things were already going wrong. Agent McClaren managed to evade his guard during one of the steam bursts the engine would let out while stopped. McClaren ran back to the church to raise the alarm. Not many citizens were armed, but they headed towards the depot all the same.

At that same time another man noticed one of the masked robbers jumping from the express car. He watched as the masked man was joined by a second, and the two ran for their horses. The man may have been at home, in one of the houses that stood near the depot. He ran onto the scene with a gun in his hand. It was pitch dark, so rather than trying to aim for the robbers, the brave citizen fired at the horses. He killed one of the villains' steeds.

Now everyone was alerted to situation. The few citizens from the ice-cream social who had guns began firing. The criminals doubled up on the one horse still alive. As they headed south out of town one man returned fire. One of his shots hit home; 38-year-old William Benford had a bullet in his spine.

The next day the *Wichita Daily Eagle* told the story of the train robbery. "Frisco Is Held Up," the piece began. It offered descriptions of the two men: one was short and stocky, the other "tall, spare but muscular." It speculated that the two may have been responsible for post office robberies in Crystal Springs and Danville (in Kansas) that had occurred in the last month. There was also mention of the creamery checks being canceled.

The next issue of the *Eagle* to add more details was Tuesday, July 19. Under the title "Are Under Arrest," the account included a report of a horse and buggy stolen from a farmer in southeastern Sedgwick County. The major news was that two men fitting the description of the criminals had been spotted in Maize. After taking precautions not to start a gunfight in the town the men were apprehended. Unfortunately the two men could not be positively identified as the Andover train robbers. A day after their arrest the men were set free. It appeared that the hand of justice would not catch the guilty men.

Then, on August the 4th, news came from the town of Nowata, Oklahoma Territory, south of Coffeyville. Two men, Samuel Smith and Tom Wynn (or Winn), had been taken into custody on suspicion of robbing the Frisco train at Andover. Wynn was from the Indian Territory, and was either a half-breed or full-blooded Indian, with a criminal record. He met Smith in the Lansing prison, and they'd escaped together in the early part of the summer of 1898.

Smith was a far more unpleasant character. The previous year he'd carried on a reign of terror in Cowley and Sumner Counties. He would ride up to isolated farm houses and demand the family's valuables, threatening to shoot the women and children if not satisfied. Smith had been wounded in the Andover robbery, but not seriously, and hid at his father-in-law's house near Belle Plaine for a short time. When he was captured Smith was disguised as a clergyman, and tried to shake off his pursuers first by shooting at them, then by hiding in a mud-hole.

Smith and Wynn would be tried in El Dorado. Marshal Sid Blakeman of Leon, aided by an unnamed Wells Fargo agent, went south to bring the men back to Butler County. There was no direct rail line from Coffeyville to El Dorado, so they took a complicated route. They traveled from southeastern Kansas to the Frisco line, took a train into Wichita, then took a Missouri Pacific train to El Dorado. This would take Smith and Wynn through Andover.

The scene in Andover as the train pulled into town can well be imagined. Anyone who had gun probably carried it. There was talk of lynchings and other acts of "frontier justice." Angry shouts and cries could have been heard inside the car. A few people were brought on board to identify Smith and Wynn as the robbers. The stop was short, the men and their escorts continued on, and they arrived in El Dorado on Monday, August 8, 1898.

The two accused felons spent the next few months in the El Dorado jail under heavy guard. Depot Agent McClaren was brought in, and positively identified Smith and Wynn. Smith's family hired a lawyer from the Kansas City area to represent him. The actual charges against the men were held up until the condition of Will Benford, the only man seriously wounded in the robbery, was resolved.

On August 22 Benford died. He was shot in the spine, and had been paralyzed. To this day it remains unclear under what circumstances Benford received his mortal wound. An early report of the holdup said that an unarmed man had tried to stop the robbers and was gravely wounded. Later reports suggest that Benford was hit in the general melee that occurred as Smith and Wynn fled town.

However it happened, it was ascertained that Smith had fired the fatal shot. In November of 1898 Smith was convicted of first-degree murder and sentenced to death by hanging. Wynn was convicted of second-degree murder, sentenced to 20 years, and both were sent back to Lansing.

Smith tried to escape his death sentence two years later. His attempt was an utter failure. He was shot by prison guards, and subsequently died of his wounds. Wynn successfully escaped in November 1912. He was recaptured three months later, but was set free in 1914 when the governor commuted his sentence. Wynn was not seen in Kansas again; it's likely he returned to Oklahoma and lived out his life there.

Changes continued to occur in Andover as the memories of the Frisco robbery faded. The blacksmith shop where the bandits tied their horses was torn down in the 1910's and the Andover State Bank built its first building on the site. Depot Agent McClaren remained in Andover, and later owned the town's lumberyard. The Frisco depot stood for a long time, serving the town's freight and passenger traffic. When the Frisco ended all passenger service in 1960 the depot was abandoned. It was almost saved by the Great Plains Transportation Museum in Wichita, but terms weren't agreed upon, and the depot was torn down and lost.

An old church stands not far from where the events of that July day took place. It was the Methodist church, but it may not have been "the" church. The original Andover Methodist church building was destroyed, and another church building moved in. The dates of this move aren't yet known, so the question of whether that building played a part in this story remains unanswered.

The only building from that era that still exists is the old general store building. The store's indented doorway served as a haven for those trying to hide from the bandits' bullets. It might have been where Will Benford was first taken. Citizens buying good there no doubt talked of the crime for weeks. The store is now under threat of demolition by the City of Andover, for being old and in disrepair.

A few questions about the men who held up the train have yet to answered. Did they know about the ice-cream social? Was it a part of their plan? Did they hope that, with everyone at the church, no one would see them robbing the train?

If they were taking the social into consideration, it would seem that they were counting on too much. If the social had not been occurring, McClaren would not have had any place to escape to or a convenient crowd to rally. Indeed, if there had not been a social, the townspeople would have been fast asleep during the robbery.

If they didn't know about that ice-cream social, then Smith and Wynn made a serious miscalculation. They chose the wrong place and the wrong time. The first thing that went wrong brought the mob. The mob saw the villains, and that great number of witnesses sealed their fate. It was this error that eventually ended Smith's life, and kept Wynn in prison for almost fourteen years.

In the end, it was that error in the timing of their crime that brought them to justice. It was that error that kept the act from being an unsolved mystery. It was that error that distinguishes the Andover train robbery from all others, before and since.

Postscript: In the mid-1990s the general store building was torn down despite an effort by the local historical society to save it. In 1995 Burlington Northern merged with the Atchison, Topeka & Santa Fe to form Burlington Northern Santa Fe. Around 2000 BNSF sold the line from Andover to Augusta to Butler County. The county government was unable to find an operator to service the line, and the track was removed half a dozen years later.

TROLLEY TO THE OIL FIELDS:
The Wichita-Walnut Valley Interurban Project

Over the course of several months in 1917 an "interurban railroad" was the talk of Sedgwick and Butler Counties. It was proposed as a link between Wichita and the oil fields of El Dorado and Augusta. It was backed by powerful men and a great deal of money.

But no route was graded, no rail was laid, and no trolleys ran. The project has become lost to history, with only newspaper accounts to record its promise. But for a time the Wichita-Walnut Valley Interurban was buoyed by high hopes and strong support.

As the Twentieth Century began the transportation method of the future appeared to be the "interurban" railroad. Interurban cars were powered by electricity from overhead lines connected to a power plant. Trains on so-called "steam railroads" needed a locomotive with its own power, namely steam from a boiler to move pistons that turned wheels. Interurban trains, on the other hand, didn't need a locomotive and could consist of a single car.

This meant that interurbans didn't need wide-radius curves to accommodate large locomotives. They could operate on, over, or under city streets and county roads. The hope was that interurbans would be able to serve the modest freight and passenger needs of smaller communities; could link cramped industries to steam railroads; and would allow workers to get to their jobs without having to live close to their workplaces.

In the Wichita area this trend that led to the creation of the Arkansas Valley Interurban, or AVI. Founded in the early 1900's, the AVI was backed by some of the wealthiest men of Wichita and supported by the city's two newspapers and many civic boosters. An aggressive investment campaign started in 1909 was followed by track-laying in 1910. By November of that year the AVI's first intercity service had begun between Wichita and Valley Center.

A month later operations were extended to Sedgwick. Lack of investment from Newton held up construction for a short time. That city was reached in October of 1911, followed by Halstead in December. An extension of the Newton line was built up to Bethel College in 1913. Work resumed at Halstead in 1915, and in December the AVI was completed to Hutchinson.

From the start ridership on the AVI was significant. Over 30,000 people a month rode AVI trolleys in 1911, and by 1917 the monthly average was around 65,000. The company had to increase departures and arrivals from every two hours to hourly to handle the passengers. Considering this volume it isn't hard to make the same logical leap that the supporters of the Wichita-Walnut Valley made in 1917. The Butler County oil boom was bringing in both people and money. If the AVI was doing well serving the quiet communities to the north of Wichita, how well could the W-WV do running trolleys to the oil fields?

This was on the minds of the interurban's backers when they gathered in the Innes Tea Room in Wichita on April 14, 1917. At the meeting were several prominent Wichitans, Dr. H. A. Hill of Augusta, and Charles Galligan of El Dorado. They organized the railroad as the "Wichita-Walnut Valley Interurban Railway Company" with an initial capitalization of $1,000,000. J. H. Butts was elected president, T. C. Coffman secretary, and L. S. Naftzger treasurer.

Two routes to El Dorado were put under consideration. One would head east from Wichita to Augusta and up to El Dorado; the second would run northeast through Andover, Benton, and Towanda. By early May route plans were changed to an El Dorado branch and an Augusta-Douglass branch.

The latter branch may also reflect the influence of the AVI itself. The year before the *Wichita Beacon* had reported that the road was planning to extend its lines east to Augusta and south to Wellington and Winfield. AVI General Manager Robert Campbell had said that the east plans were being made because of oil and gas discoveries and "a strong demand for the closest possible touch between Wichita and the towns in that district."

This sentiment was repeated a year later when the W-WV was created. The *Wichita Eagle* of April 16, 1917, reported that businessmen traveling between Wichita and the Butler fields were unhappy with the current situation. The greatest trouble was clearly in the winter, when it seems the only option was a long, cold automobile ride on inadequate roads.

The omission of the Missouri Pacific in the story implied that train trips were inconvenient. A glance at a May 1917 public timetable backs that up. There were only two eastbound and two westbound passenger trains. Both west trains left El Dorado between 8:00 and

8:30 in the morning. One of the east trains arrived just before 11:00 AM, while the other came into El Dorado half an hour before midnight. Clearly it was difficult to travel between Wichita and El Dorado in one day by steam railroad. Putting the W-WV into operation promised to correct that problem.

Optimism marked the founding of the interurban. President Butts told the *Eagle* that rails could be bought within six months, and that the W-WV would only use "high-class rolling stock." The *Beacon* reported that officials believed both routes would eventually be built, with construction of one certain in the immediate future.

The next steps carried out by the W-WV backers were a series of meetings with citizens of El Dorado, Augusta, and Douglass. The first story in the *El Dorado Daily Republican* on April 16 said that prominent El Doradans supported the project. But four days later the *Weekly Republican* reported opposition by people who believed that the road would make stop oil men from continuing to reside in their smaller city. Countering this, the editor of the *Republican* wrote that if El Dorado had a large and attractive hotel people would come there instead of visiting Wichita, and an interurban would make that hotel project more likely.

The other newspaper in town, the *Walnut Valley Times*, was not so favorable to the interurban. It published two stories on the W-WV in the daily issue of April 16. One focused on the hotel effort the *Republican* had referred to. The other predicted the interurban would not be a success by claiming that its backers were inexperienced and that investment would be slow in coming. The second story concluded by echoing the anti-Wichita sentiment that the *Republican* reported on April 20.

Stronger support for the W-WV came from Douglass. On April 25 twelve members of the town's Commercial Club traveled to Wichita to meet with the W-WV officers. The Douglass men were told that the line would run east to the county line and there split into two branches, one to El Dorado and one to Douglass.

Sentiment here decidedly favored the new interurban. The *Douglass Tribune* of April 27 said that the new railroad would "fill a long felt want." The Commercial Club held a second meeting to discuss the project. Although the Club felt the amount of stock requested of them was too high, it still supported the effort. Support continued to be expressed in the newspaper through May with a proposal for a specific route into town.

The secretary of the Club, J. A. Clay, wrote a regular column for the Tribune on Club projects and views. At the end of the month Clay encouraged his community to back the W-WV interurban. The town needed better connections with the "outside world," and this was their chance. Only community backing would make the road a reality. Club members who traveled to Valley Center to investigate the impact

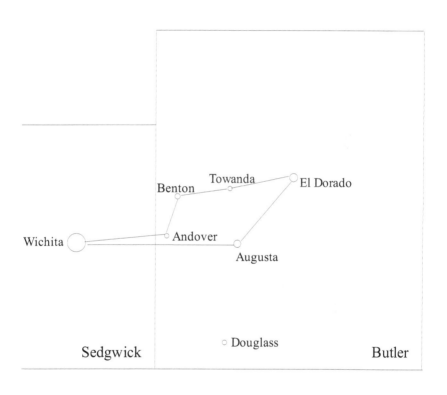

W&WV,
Initial Route

of the AVI found benefits, Clay reported. Business up there was better and more homes had been built.

"It is our opportunity," Clay concluded. "The money is here and we need the road. Shall we get busy and secure it?"

Attention now shifted to Augusta. The May 2 issue of the *Daily Gazette* carried a front-page announcement for the interurban meeting at the Chamber of Commerce. Other topics were on the agenda, but it was the interurban that seemed to be the most important. "Do not leave the attendance at this meeting to some other man," the author wrote. "You will be well repaid."

The next day's issue reported on the meeting. The W-WV backers explained their plans. Augustans were encouraged to help secure a right of way, vote bonds, and make stock subscriptions. The story concluding by saying that the attendees agreed "that such a road would be a great step toward development of the rich Walnut Valley."

In that same issue the editor of the *Gazette*, Glen E. Kiser, expressed a somewhat obvious opinion about the interurban. "If the scheme is one of purely promotion," he wrote, "Augusta wants none of it. If it is bona fide, it will benefit the city."

The *Republican's* take on Augusta's feelings were more positive. It described the meeting as "rousing." It said the Mayor was "heartily in favor of the project." It added that a pioneer settler of Augusta knew President Butts and would therefore support any project that Butts was attached to.

When word from the interurban camp suggested that the junction point between the Douglass and El Dorado branches might be placed two miles west of Augusta, Kiser turned unfriendly. He hinted that the W-WV backers weren't trying to boost Augusta after all. He said that Douglass was "off on the wrong foot" by continuing to support the project.

Kiser might have ate a little crow in early June. One of the interurban's promoters came to Augusta on June 8. Charles Payne was quoted as saying that three-quarters of the right of way between that town and Wichita was secured. He added that Augusta would indeed be the junction. Plans now called for one branch south to Douglass and a second that would go through Towanda to reach El Dorado.

Hard news about the W-WV faded as America geared up to enter World War One. J. A. Clay in Douglass was upbeat on the project in June, saying that it wasn't dead and still needed community support. Things remained quiet until late July when word came out of an important development.

On July 20 W-WV Chairman Charles Galligan announced that the road had obtained a right of way. The company had all but secured its line from Wichita to Augusta. Negociations would continue to complete the right of way, then start on a route through Haverhill to El Dorado. Galligan predicted that work on the grade would start in September.

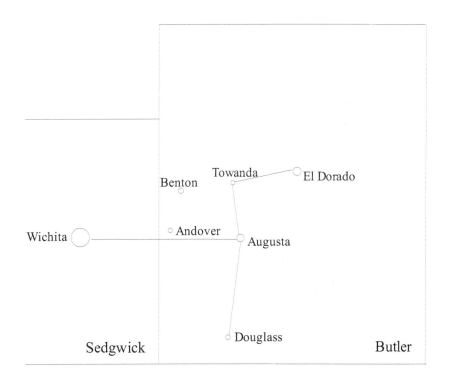

W&WV,
June 1917 Route

Down in Douglass no one seemed bothered by the announcement. But later in August the *Tribune* reported that Butts had visited the town and had assured locals that the trolleys would come. On August 10 Clay wrote that interurban backers had promised a train running to town each hour from six in the morning to eleven at night. On the 31st Clay predicted that construction would start "before long."

Then on September 5, 1917, the state charter board granted a charter to W-WV with capital stock of $2,000,000. Construction was set to begin on October 1 on the Wichita-El Dorado route. Predictions were that trains would be running within a year. Treasurer L. S. Naftzger reported that $300,000 worth of stock was already sold. Naftzger added that all of the stock would be owned locally. It was also announced that the right of way south to Douglass was also almost completely secured.

Opinions on this development are hard to gauge. The *Gazette* reported the story without comments, while the *Republican* seemed upbeat. The *Walnut Valley Times* also didn't comment, but its report was only the second time it had written about the W-WV. Curiously the only news in the *Tribune* about the interurban's charter was in Clay's Commercial Club column.

The *Tribune* was the main source of news on the project for the next two months. In late September it reported that the surveyors were laying out the actual right of way. That same day a backer told the *Gazette*, "Things could not be moving along better." A month later the *Tribune* said the surveyors were taking the interurban into Douglass west of the Santa Fe's line. On November 2 the *Tribune* detailed the W-WV's exact route into the community.

That same issue contained J. A. Clay's biggest news yet for the interurban. He wrote that the surveyors had continued on south to Winfield. He added that backers of an interurban that ran from Kansas City to Lawrence were prepared to extend their line through Topeka to Emporia. They had asked the W-WV group to build north from El Dorado to Emporia and link the two systems.

It's unlikely that this ambitious alliance would have ever gotten off the ground. It would have required a massive investment in capital, construction materials, and operating equipment. The Kansas City-Topeka end of the system would have to compete with not one but three steam railroads: the Santa Fe; the Union Pacific; and the Rock Island (which had trackage rights on the UP). The whole system would be competing mainly with the Santa Fe and tangentially with the Missouri Pacific.

Nothing more was heard from the W-WV camp on this or anything else until the end of December. On December 21 it was announced that the Scott Construction Company of St. Louis would be building the W-WV. The route would be mapped out and work would start in January. The line would now run out of Wichita along Twenty-First Street to Andover where it would split into an Augusta branch and an El Dorado branch. The former would also serve Douglass and Winfield, while the latter would run through Benton and Towanda.

The *Gazette* was unhappy with these route changes and said so. The *Republican* said nothing, merely quoting some of what the Wichita *Eagle* wrote. There was no story in the *Walnut Valley Times*, not surprising considering its early skepticism. What is surprising is that the *Tribune*, long the strongest supporter of the interurban project in Butler County, didn't even devote one line to this news.

Almost six weeks passed before there was any more news about the project. Then on February 13, 1918, the state's public utilities commission approved the W-WV's application to issue some $1.2 million in stock. It didn't get the $2 million it had asked for. Backers seemed confident enough that construction would finally get started in the spring.

But that was the last positive news from the Wichita-Walnut Valley Interurban. The final survey wasn't carried out, no roadbed was graded, and no tracks were laid.

The most likely explanation for the failure of the project is a simple one: the First World War. Construction material would have been hard to come by once America began mass-producing guns and ships for the war effort. With the federal government taking over operation of the steam railroads, any rail produced would probably have been allocated to upgrade important steam lines. This project would have to wait its turn, especially since it proposed to serve oil fields already served by steam roads. Just as important is the fact that the drive to sell war bonds would have removed much of the available capital needed to purchase construction material and operating equipment.

Another factor operating against the interurban project was the rise of the automobile. Next to the stories about the W-WV were reports of meetings calling for permanent paved roads in Butler County. This "good roads movement" was gaining strength here as it was across the state and

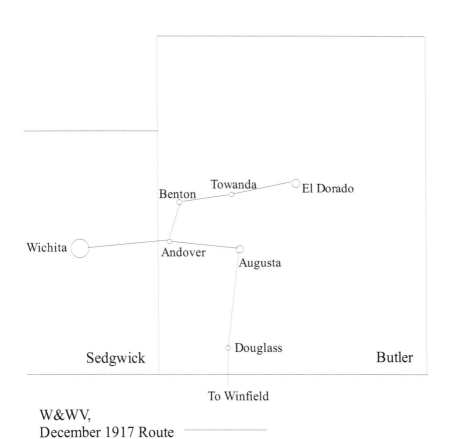

Towanda

El Dorado

Benton

Wichita

Andover

Augusta

Douglass

Sedgwick

Butler

To Winfield

W&WV,
December 1917 Route

around the nation. When these roads became a reality after the War passenger traffic on the Arkansas Valley Interurban dropped steadily. The tide was turning against the W-WV's backers almost from the start.

An attempt to revive the stalled interurban was tried in the summer of 1920. This time the W-WV would bypass El Dorado and Augusta. Instead it would run through Douglass to Winfield. It would take over the existing Southwestern Interurban between Winfield and Arkansas City, and continue into Oklahoma with lines to Guthrie and Enid. But instead of trolley-type electric cars this road would operate with motor cars, probably similar to the "doodlebugs" the steam railroads used. One meeting about the project was held in early July and some $21,000 was invested from Andover, Douglass, and Rose Hill. But nothing more was heard about the effort, and the whole idea was soon forgotten.

So ends the story of the attempt to build an electric railroad to the Butler County oil fields. But as we use up more of that irreplaceable oil driving between Wichita and Butler County, it's possible that the history of Wichita-Walnut Valley Interurban isn't over. Maybe the project wasn't behind its time, but well ahead of its time.

There could yet be a trolley in Butler County's future.

OTTO P. BYERS:
A KANSAS RAILROAD MAN

The dream of every employee is usually to rise from their low standing to president of the company, or better yet to take charge of a competing company. Few actually get to realize this dream. But one man, Otto Byers, was able to work his way up the railroad industry from mere section hand to president of the Anthony & Northern Railroad.

Byers seems to have been dedicated to railroading and his home state. He worked for one line or another from the age of 15 up to his death in 1933. He wrote a handful of articles on his experiences and knowledge of the industry. He even had a town named for him.

None of this could have been forecast for Otto Phillip Byers when he was born on May 2, 1863, in Tampico, Indiana. He was the son of a doctor serving in the Union Army. He had one brother, James. Sadly his mother died when Otto was only two years old. Byers stayed in school until he was fourteen. He spent at least a year at work in Indiana, perhaps in the timber business.

On August 29, 1878, Byers turned up at Brookville, Kansas. Within two weeks he had hired on as a section hand for the Kansas Pacific railroad. He would have found a railroad in rough shape. A decade before, as the Union Pacific Eastern Division, the road had struggled to be first to build across the state. The late 1860's had seen a boom in prosperity thanks to Texas cattle driven up to Abilene and shipped east on the KP. But those drives stopped coming to Abilene after 1872, and the road was now a decrepit pawn between speculator Jay Gould and the management of the Union Pacific.

As section hand he was part of a "section crew" responsible for track maintenance. Section crews would replace damaged track, ties, and grades. Crews might also construct lines, either building new lines or adding sidings to existing routes. It was hard work on the low end of railroading's totem pole.

Although Byers came late to the KP, he seems to have known the character of the road in its earlier days. His last article for the Kansas State Historical Society was on the road. He wrote about the tough men who worked on the line, the Indian attacks of the 1860's, and passengers shooting buffalo from trains.

He took a few paragraphs to write about the "box relay" system used at the time to keep work crews informed of Indian raids. A telegrapher was assigned to a train with the specific job of connecting his relay to the telegraph wires when orders were needed. Trains weren't even allowed to depart unless a telegrapher could be found.

It's the sort of information that would either come from experience or from talking to experienced men. One can easily imagine the teenaged Byers listening to the tales of grizzled veterans during lulls or after hours. They must have made quite an impression for him to be able to write about those memories fifty years later with a tone of fond nostalgia.

When the Union Pacific took over the KP in 1880 Byers stayed with the new owner. Here his rise up the employment ladder begins in earnest. By the time he left the UP in 1887 he had been a brakeman, a station agent, a trainmaster, and a dispatcher. His postings carried him all over the old KP from his start at Brookville. Over that nine-year period he lived in McPherson, Carbondale, Wamego, St. Mary's, Solomon, and Abilene. He must have risen quickly, for in later years he claimed to have been a brakeman on the train that carried part of the Seventh Cavalry to the trail of Dull Knife following his raid through western Kansas in the fall of 1878.

Each of the jobs he held carried certain responsibilities. Being a brakeman was by far the most dangerous. The brakeman was the man who had to physically stop or slow the train. In the days before the air brake in the locomotive, this often meant climbing on top of cars to turn the brake wheel. Brakemen could lose their lives being thrown from a train, or by being crushed between cars. It's amazing that he survived this duty.

His next three positions indicate that Byers had some ability for record-keeping and management. The most visible of the three was station agent, which he seems to have served at more than one station. The agent was the railroad employee that most of the public had contact with. For many small communities, the agent was the railroad.

The station agent was responsible for ordering freight cars for local customers and for getting smaller freight shipments delivered, whether those were dresses or farm implements. He would take the mail bag from the station to the post office. He would sell passenger tickets. He manned the telegraph, and would therefore be first to get news from the personal to the national. Without his diligence a community would be in dire trouble.

The agent also had duties to the railroad as well as to the town he worked in. If something happened, from a culvert washout to a train robbery, the agent had to pass that information along. He also had to keep his superiors informed of train delays caused by extra work or maintenance problems. Train crews would look to the agent to pass along updates to their standing orders. These tasks had him working closely with dispatchers, and it's likely through this that Byers next moved up.

A dispatcher was posted at a division or sub-division point along a line. His duty was to keep track of train movements along his territory and insure that trains did not collide. derail, or suffer some other disaster. He would send special orders to station agents and train crews via telegraph to cope with every situation. Railroads operated well with this system until the development of two-way portable radio communications after World War Two.

His final position, trainmaster, was the superior to the dispatchers. The trainmaster was responsible for the safe operation of trains in his territory. He was also the man who made certain his train crews followed their rules and schedules. Crewmen would broke the rules would have to come before the trainmaster and face his judgment.

In July of 1887 Byers left the UP and became an employee of the Chicago, Rock Island & Pacific. His first job was as a telegraph operator with a track layering crew. His first posting was on the Rock Island's Salina branch. This might have been when he was at Abilene, and could explain how he moved from the UP to the RI. That year the RI entered Kansas in a big way, crisscrossing the state with main lines.

The chance to open new routes may have appealed to Byers. The years 1887 and 1888 would later prove to be the last big railroad boom in Kansas. Byers later moved to the crews laying track to Liberal on what would later be called the "Golden State Route." It's also possible that Byers was trying to gain favor with RI management. He must have made some impression, because he soon became an agent in Hutchinson.

At Hutchinson Byers would get his first taste of being in charge of a railroad. The latter half of the 1880's saw UP management interested in constructing a new main line south to the Gulf of Mexico. The project would begin by extending the Salina-McPherson branch through Hutchinson to Kingman. A company was formed and investment got under way.

The segment from McPherson to Hutchinson was similar to the route the RI was building to Liberal. The two railroads came to an agreement that would allow them to exchange trackage rights. This would let UP trains run on the RI from McPherson to Hutchinson. That meant construction of that segment was now unnecessary.

Months later a change in management at the UP led to renunciation of the trackage agreement and disinterest in the Gulf project. One prominent Hutchinson man was interested in the project, and he convinced the UP to give him the project's franchise. Aiding the local man were three men from Chicago, one being the brother-in-law of famed general John Schofield.

Another of the three was the general manager of the Rock Island. It's likely that Otto Byers played an important role in making this connection. The best evidence is the fact that when directors and officers of the new railroad were elected in March of 1889 Byers was made superintendent.

The line from Hutchinson to Kingman was built in 1889. Another change in UP management led to a renewed interest in the effort. That alliance led to track being laid from Kingman through Anthony to the state border in 1890. UP leadership then changed again, repudiated the project, and left the company in the hands of its builders. The Hutchinson & Southern struggled to stay afloat during the 1890's. It eventually failed and at the end of 1899 it became part of the Santa Fe.

In March of 1901 Byers returned to the Rock Island. He was made the division freight agent in Hutchinson. At this same time the RI had decided to extend its line from Liberal down to El Paso, Texas. The lure of seeing a new railroad laid out attracted Byers again, and he joined the construction crew carrying out his duties as they worked.

By Christmas 263 miles of track were laid to Santa Rosa, New Mexico, the RI connected with the Southern Pacific. This joint RI-SP line would become known as the "Golden State Route" connecting Los Angeles and Chicago. Once it was finished Byers returned to Hutchinson and stayed a Rock Island employee until December of 1905.

At that point he moved away from the railroad industry to become general agent for a wholesale coal business based in New Mexico. He also came to invest in a flour mill in Pratt, Kansas. It was this investment, and his love of railroading, that brought him back as a company president.

Byers began to consider building a railroad that would run from

Iuka, north of Pratt, southeast to Anthony. His idea was to offer farmers in the area an alternate route to get their grain to the Gulf of Mexico. The Missouri Pacific offered the only such route, and as such could set its own shipping rates. Byers' road would connect at Anthony to the Kansas City, Mexico & Orient, and give those farmers an option. But in the back of Byers' mind was that this would also be his chance to become president of a railroad.

Byers came together with a group of supporters and in late 1912 created the Anthony & Northern. Construction began in 1913 with a line built from Iuka to the Rock Island line at Pratt. At this point the A&N changed direction. Farmers in northern Pratt County were willing to vote bonds to get a railroad to ship their grain. The group looked west and found an area where many farms were five to ten miles from the nearest track. In the era before the auto, this was a considerable distance to haul grain wagons to a grain elevator.

The direction of the A&N was changed from southeast to west, a right-of-way surveyed, and construction resumed. About eight miles west of Iuka a town came into existence along the road called Byers. Named for the new road's president, the town of Byers grew quickly. At its peak the railroad served a couple of grain elevators, a lumber yard, and a bulk oil dealers in Byers. It wasn't the biggest or most important town on the line, but no doubt Byers was proud of the community that bore his name.

The A&N was completed to Kinsley in 1916. At the village of Trousdale in southeastern Edwards County a second line was built north. It was supposed to go to Hays, but stopped twenty miles northwest of Larned at a village called Vaughn. Materials were on hand for further construction, but the start of World War One halted work. The A&N was more or less done.

Operating with a variety of used locomotives and eclectic equipment, the A&N did well for a few years. All along its lines grain elevators were built so farmers could bring harvested crops there. The railroad would pick up loaded cars and ship those crops to the wider world. The road's name was changed in 1919 to "Wichita Northwestern" in the hope of extending its line east to Kansas' largest city and increasing its traffic. Also part of Byers' empire was the Kansas & Oklahoma, a line that crept north from Liberal and had traffic similar to the A&N.

As the A&N was getting started Byers began writing about Kansas. The impetus of this isn't known, but it might date back to his earliest days on the Kansas Pacific. He certainly heard tales about the struggle of that road to cross the state. Perhaps after the turn of the century someone asked Byers to relate some of his experiences. It may also be that he saw relating the history he had witnessed as an ideal method of promoting his projects.

Sometime before 1912 he compiled an article for the Kansas State Historical Society about the legendary blizzard that crippled Kansas in January of 1886. Actually a series of storms following one after another, "the blizzard" almost destroyed the state's cattle industry; killed dozens of settlers; and left the state buried under inches of snow. And coming after a drought that had all but ruined Kansas farmers, the storm devastated the state's economy.

Byers was a UP employee at the time. In the article he explains the many ways the storm affected the state's railroads. He tells of cuts drifting shut, of men having to hand-clear the tracks, and of experienced engineers failing to see depots due to what we now call "white-outs." Reading this piece it's clear that Byers himself was pressed into road clearing service. No doubt he was somewhat thankful that, unlike most front-office men, he had experience with hard work under rough conditions.

Byers didn't simply write on the blizzard's impact on railroads. He tells of several instances of people becoming lost. He devotes much space to the financial losses suffered by cattlemen. He includes diary entries from a man who spent seven days getting from Kansas City to Meade; an account from Henry Inman's book about Buffalo Jones; and excerpts from western Kansas newspapers. Also part of the article is a Topeka newspaper story on a winter storm that hit Dodge City in 1885 and a first-person piece on an 1856 storm.

Not too long after this article Byers wrote a brief history of the Hutchinson & Southern for the state historical society. His knowledge of the personalities involved and the road's roller coaster relationship with the Union Pacific demonstrates that he had a keen interest in the project. But he only mentions his part once, when he recounts the 1889 election of officers.

About ten years later he wrote about his experiences on the Rock Island. Inadvertently published in the **Kansas Historical Collections** (the society's irregularly-issued volume of speeches and articles) under the name "Oliver Philip Byers," this article mainly focused on construction of the "Golden State Route." He mentions the county-seat wars that occurred in Pratt and Seward Counties and a bond default scandal in Stevens County.

His story then turns to the El Paso extension. Here again he shows his passion for railroading. As he describes the hardships of building this line, including disease, vice, and desert animals, he clearly wants his reader to sympathize with the workers. He wants them to admire the dedication of those who stayed till the end. He praises the men who supervised the construction crews and the locomotive engineers who ran their trains on the line without benefit of telegraph communications.

As was mentioned earlier, his last article published in the **Collections** was about the Kansas Pacific. Called "When Railroading Outdid The Wild West Stories," it appeared in 1928 but had first been published in Union Pacific's magazine two years earlier.

By then Byers was in his mid-60s, with much of his life behind him. The article is more of a personal reflection than a true history. He's still eager to inform, but he provides fewer dates and other facts. The passion is there, but it's more of the author than of the amateur historian.

This tone is revealed by the important episodes in the KP's story that he either briefly mentions or omits. He mentions the murder of the first driving leader of the railroad, Samuel Hallett, but leaves out the fascinating details of the crime. He says nothing about the struggle between Jay Gould and the UP that ended the KP's independence. Nor does he mention the most famous part of the road's history, its role as destination of the cattle drives to Abilene.

When it comes to the construction of the main line from Kansas City to Denver, Byers first takes the reader from the start in the early 1860's to completion in 1870. He then backs up to tell of Indian raids the construction crews had to deal with in 1867 and 1868.

The main raid story he writes about is of an attack on Brookville. He gives no dates, and doesn't say much more about any other attack. The surprising aspect is that while the Brookville story is interesting, the story isn't as marked to history as is the raid at present-day Victoria. The latter has a cemetery that survives, while the former doesn't.

He takes some sentences, even a paragraph or two, to show what railroading was like on the frontier. He tells of the link-and-pin coupler system; the rough workers who hid their identities; and the terribly slow speeds of freight and passenger trains. He hails the hardy pioneers who settled along the KP, but gets wrong the fact of which

Germans emigrated to villages along the line. It was "Volga German" Catholics, instead of the Mennonites that Byers stated (they moved along the Santa Fe's lines).

Despite these errors and quirks, Byers' effort was a good one. The Kansas Pacific was on track to become forgotten, or mistaken for being part of the famed Union Pacific. The frontier was long gone and its realities were turning into legends and myths. Railroading had changed from risky and "make do" to a large and standardized industry. Byers gives his readers a glimpse of the past as it was.

He also reveals some of himself in this article. Towards the end of his narrative he describes the KP as "the writer's first love and its territory his boyhood home." Fifty years after arriving in the state, Otto Byers was a firm Kansan. He had strong roots planted in the soil. He appreciated the state's history, and was eager to share his small part in it with others.

He might also have wanted a brief respite from a present that was turning increasingly harsh.

By the late 1920's the realities of running a small railroad centered around rural agriculture was catching up to Byers and company he presided over. An economic downturn after the War led to the Wichita Northwestern falling into receivership in 1922. Byers and his assistant had been appointed receivers, but the former assistant died in 1925. Traffic on the road ran hot and cold during the decade, with peaks in both passenger and freight coming around 1928.

The Great Depression hurt the WNW's financial picture, but the damage was limited due the road's already rough shape. What would eventually kill the line was the "Dust Bowl" that created crop failures, and the use of trucks to haul grain from farms to elevators in surrounding county-seat cities. Without that grain the reason for the operation of the WNW ceased to exist.

Late in 1933 citizens along the WNW tried to interest the Rock Island in purchasing the line to maintain service. RI management at the time seemed at best ambivalent, although they did inspect the line. T. A. Fry, the receiver, tried to further help the WNW by getting the Federal government to pay some $13,000 that he felt the railroad was owed for carrying the mail.

Otto Byers was now in Chicago, having moved there two years before. According to the *Kinsley Mercury* of November 9, he was sick and broken hearted. He was never able to recover his health, and he died on April 7, 1936. He left behind his wife, his daughter, seven grandchildren, and two great-grandchildren. His body was brought back to Hutchinson to be buried in city that had been his home for so long.

One sad aspect of his death can be seen in his article on the Hutchinson & Southern. He concluded the piece by reporting that all the builders of the railroad had died except himself. He then added, "It is rather remarkable, too, that, though each of them had made a fortune in the building and bonding of the road, this profit soon disappeared and each of them died a poor man." Byers might not have been poor in wealth at the time of his death, but he was certainly poor in spirit.

The WNW soldiered on without its founder, but everything was turning against it. Car loadings steadily dropped through the decade, with only a brief respite when it carried pipes for an oil pipeline. Maintenance was deferred, passenger traffic dried up, and abandonment finally came in 1941. Almost everything associated with the WNW is gone: the cars; locomotives; depots; even some of the villages along the line have faded away.

What does live on is the story of the railroad and the man who created it. Otto Byers may not have been born in Kansas, but he adopted the state as his home. His life spanned an amazing time in the state's history. Not only was he was there to see it, but he was able to pass on what he saw for the benefit of the Kansans who came after him.

Otto P. Byers (1863-1936), employed on several Kansas railroads, founder and president of the Anthony & Northern, and author of several articles on state railroad history. *Photo courtesy of the Kansas State Historical Society.*

Robert Collins

THE "SAMSON OF THE CIMARRON" STORY

If a railroad bridge is known at all it's because something happened there, probably something tragic or heroic, or because the bridge has architectural significance. Of course railroad bridges these days don't have quite the flair that they did a few decades ago. The railroads themselves don't have that flair like they used to. But there are some that still have a bit of magic about them.

The railroad bridge over the Cimarron River about ten miles northeast of Liberal is one of those bridges. Known as the "Samson of the Cimarron," it's the only one in Kansas to have a park close to that allows visitors to view it. It's thought to be the longest bridge over a dry river in the country. The story behind the Samson of the Cimarron is one of luck, misfortune, and pride.

The story begins in the late 1880's as the Chicago, Rock Island & Pacific railroad undertook a massive expansion. At the end of 1885 the "Rock Island" formed a construction company, the Chicago, Kansas & Nebraska, to build some 700 miles of lines through both states. One of those lines extended southwest from Topeka through Hutchinson to Liberal on the southern Kansas border. The goal of this route was El Paso, Texas, but before construction could continue the Rock Island needed government permission to enter Oklahoma Territory. It took a few years but the railroad was allowed to continue southwest. The tracks eventually reached Santa Rose, New Mexico, where a connection was made with the Southern Pacific.

This connection yielded a route from Chicago to Los Angeles, soon called the "Golden State Route." It allowed the two railroads to compete with the Atchison, Topeka & Santa Fe for freight and passenger traffic between the cities. The Rock Island entered the Twentieth Century as one of the major railroads of the midwestern United States.

Unfortunately this led to problems with the company's owners. Railroad owners in those days were often tempted to use their company stock not only to increase their wealth, but to use it to take over other railroads and build empires. This happened to the Rock Island in the years before World War One and led to the company entering receivership in 1915. Incredibly it happened again in the

1920's, and again it led to financial ruin during the Great Depression.

To put an end to the chaos John Farrington was put in charge of the Rock Island. Farrington brought streamlined passenger trains to the railroad, the famed "Rock Island Rockets." He also had the road rebuild various lines that were in disrepair. The Golden State Route was chief among Farrington's efforts, and the trackage around the Cimarron River the focus of attention.

The Rock Island's tracks wound up towards the river then curved down again before straightening out on the run to Liberal. Trains had to creep slowly around these bends, and that held back the speed of traffic. The bridge over the river was an additional problem. The first bridge built was washed out in one of the Cimarron's occasional flash floods in 1914. The second one was not quite up to the demands of a modern railroad. The final impetus for change came on the morning of August 18, 1938.

The "Gold Ball" was one of the Rock Island's priority freight trains. It came up on the bridge at about 30 miles an hour, slow for such an important train but probably typical of the allowed running speed on this section. To protect approaching trains from danger, the railroad had installed an automatic blocking system to warn crews if the rails were gone. Heavy rains had brought the Cimarron River up and given it a strong current. The current was able to damage or destroy the pilings that supported the bridge. But the water hadn't yet taken out the bridge, so as the Gold Ball came up the crew in the locomotive saw a green light.

At 3:17 AM one of the largest of the Rock Island's steam locomotives crashed through the Cimarron bridge. The weight of the train was too much for the weakened structure. The locomotive and the first dozen freight cars plunged into the river. Engineer Walter Walker, fireman Carl Powell, and brakeman E. E. Holder was in the locomotive's cab. Rear brakeman C. H. Inman and the conductor were in the caboose. Also riding the train were several transients, including 18-year-old Gene Simpson from Cheney, Kansas.

Walker, Powell, and Holder fell along with their locomotive into the river. Walker and Holder were able to swim to safety, but Powell was trapped in the cab. Simpson and his fellow hobos were also thrown into the water. Simpson popped up near to where Walker and Holder were, and they told him of Powell's situation. Simpson went back under, freed Powell from the cab, and brought him up. Once the crew was accounted for someone went to the nearby booster station owned by Panhandle-Eastern and called for help.

Walker, Holder, and Inman has sustained a variety of minor injuries. Simpson was bruised, but the exertions had left him sore. Powell was the most seriously injured, with wounds to the chest, head, right wrist, and right ankle. He had also taken water into his lungs, and some of that was tainted with oil from a wrecked tank car. Unfortunately two hobos were killed in the wreck; fortunately Powell was able to recover from his injuries.

John Farrington now had his chance to fix up the route on and near the Cimarron River. The cost of a new bridge, grade, and track would cost around $1.5 million. Farrington began a drive to scrap old material and cut other costs to find the money for the project.

Part of this economy was ordering more diesel locomotives to replace steam. Steam engines required a great deal of effort to keep them running. They worked by boiling water to create steam to move pistons that turned wheels; without water a steam engine was idle. They could only run in one direction so facilities were needed to turn them, either in the construction of Y-shaped tracks called "wyes" or in building turntables. Steam engines were picky creatures that needed to spend as much time in the locomotive shop as in service. The railroads were discovering by comparison that diesel engines could spend more time in service, needed fewer men to maintain them, and could travel farther on diesel fuel than a steam engine could on water. The Rock Island's order for diesels in 1938 made them the first Western road to obtain the new engines in a large (for that time) quantity.

Farrington was able to get the capital needed to start the Cimarron project, which was underway by the end of 1938. Grading work carried on through the winter, moving some three million cubic yards of dirt to build up the approached to the planned bridge. By March of 1939 this work was done, turning a winding 12-mile line into an eight-and-a-half-mile straight line.

Not that the construction was entirely without incident. In late October a worker on the Rock Island was killed when he fell and was run over by a loaded truck. A couple of weeks later truckers working for a local firm, which had been contracted out to assist construction, went out on strike. The strike lasted a few days before being resolved. A second strike in December lasted only a day, and after that worked seems to have proceeded smoothly.

Following the grade work came the construction of the piers and the placing of the deck truss spans that made up the bridge itself. The bridge would be placed 95 feet over the riverbed. Five deck truss spans were used, creating a bridge 1,269 feet long. This part of the construction took 85 days to complete. Finally the track was laid, and with that the bridge was ready to be opened.

The opening ceremony took place on July 8, 1939, less than eleven months after the great wreck. Train No. 13 westbound would be the first to roll over the new bridge. The first passenger for No. 13 was John Farrington himself. He was joined by several local businessmen, some Rock Island employees, and family members of some of the employees. At the head of the train was locomotive No. 4000 with George Roark as engineer and Carl Powell as fireman.

He had recovered from his wounds and was back on the job. The next day the *Southwest Times* in Liberal quoted him as saying, "I sure wanted to fire this engine today. I sorta feel like pulling the first train across the bridge will give me my revenge on the old river for what she did to me a year ago."

The locomotive Powell was on that fateful August morning had also survived. It was pulled out of the river, rebuilt, and put back into service. The men of the Rock Island took to calling that engine "the submarine." No one may know if that locomotive was able to get revenge on the Cimarron as Powell did.

As train No. 13 rolled over the new bridge, B. A. Wise of the local Coca-Cola plant dropped a bottle of the soft drink onto the rails from the platform of the observation car. This was Wise's way of christening the structure. When asked later why he didn't use champagne, he replied that he didn't have any and that anyway "Coca-Cola was better."

Within days a formal christening was held, followed by the removal of the old track and grade. Aside from the floods of the Cimarron, the only loser in the effort was the settlement of Arkalon. The village had been founded along the old line back in 1888. Its first residents included former members of Fargo Springs and Springfield, two towns that had vied for the Seward County seat and lost. Arkalon struggled to hang on despite being in an area that was sandy and hilly. The community's prospects were further damaged by the 1914 flood. Ten years before the post office had closed, and now Arkalon was completely cut off. Already fading fast, Arkalon was certain to be gone within a decade or so.

Not to disappear so quickly was the bridge. The chief engineer of the project described it as the country's fastest and largest railroad construction effort. So did the Rock Island, who almost as soon as the bridge was referring it to the "Samson of the Cimarron." It's not clear how the bridge acquired this nickname, but a likely explanation is that it was coined by the railroad's publicity department.

The "Samson of the Cimarron" outlasted the Rockets, and then outlasted the Rock Island itself. The railroad was strong and prosperous after World War Two. The Union Pacific decided it would be a suitable partner, and proposed a merger in 1964. This sparked a wave of protests and competing bids that dragged on for a decade. As the struggle crawled along maintenance on the Rock Island was deferred and labor troubles mounted. When the merger was finally approved in 1974, the Union Pacific refused to go along with it; the "Rock" was in too poor a shape.

The road went bankrupt the next year. New leadership was brought in to try to save the Rock. A new blue-white paint scheme was initiated. But the new leaders couldn't stop the failure, and the colors became known as "bankruptcy blue" and "bled white." Strikes hit the Rock in 1979, other roads were brought in to operate it, and on March 31, 1980, the Chicago, Rock Island & Pacific railroad ceased to exist.

The lines of the Rock Island were sold off to other railroads. The Southern Pacific was the logical choice to take the route that crossed the Cimarron. It and the Rock Island called this the "Golden State Route" and had long partnered in passenger and freight trains running on the line. Technically the SP used its subsidiary Cotton Belt to acquire this line.

The SP was taken over by the Denver & Rio Grande Western in 1988. For a time the locomotive rumbling over the Samson could be Southern Pacific, Cotton Belt, or D&RGW. Traffic over the line stayed strong. Most trains were "unit trains" composed of a single type of freight car carrying goods in bulk between major cities, in this case between Chicago and Los Angeles.

But the steady parade of long freights wasn't enough to keep the Southern Pacific out of financial trouble. It began a search for a suitor in the mid-1990s. Since an attempt to merge with the other railroad that had a Chicago-Los Angeles line, the Santa Fe, had failed a decade earlier, the SP opted for the Union Pacific. The planned "new owner" of the Samson in 1964 became the actual new owner in 1996.

The UP is now running about 15 trains a day over the Samson and sometimes more. The highway next to it, US-54, is one of the busiest in the state. Little of this traffic stops to consider the Samson, though a few cars pull into the roadside park and rest area near the bridge. Not many people consider this the marvel of its day as the Rock Island did back in July of 1938. But the "Samson of the Cimarron" is a marvel, a testament to the fact that there was once a "mighty fine line" called the Rock Island that refused to let a dry river slow its trains. The bridge they built continues to stand as a monument to determination, perseverance, and heroism.

THE SAGA OF THE SCOTT CITY NORTHERN RAILROAD

Some interesting ideas work and some don't. The story of the Scott City Northern railroad is one of an interesting idea that failed. The SCN lasted less than a decade. But it's creation, existence, and ultimate demise make it a railroad that should not be forgotten.

The story begins around 1910 when the Garden City, Gulf & Northern was completed between Scott City and Garden City. One of the area businessmen behind the GCG&N was B. A. McCue. The project was part of his dream to build a north-south line in western Kansas. At various times the line was to start at either Garden City or Liberal and end in St. Francis. If completed the line would have connected the Chicago, Burlington & Quincy; the Rock Island; the Union Pacific; the Missouri Pacific; and the Atchison, Topeka & Santa Fe railroads.

The dream would be going against the grain. Since the Kansas Pacific had completed its line to Denver in 1870, the prevailing direction of railroad routes on the high plains was east-west. Because of this McCue's plan seems foolish on the face of it. But there was some logic in the idea, since the line would be connected to the major railroads of western Kansas. In theory the towns along its route would have greater options for its shippers in allowing them to choose where their products went, instead of going where their only railroad connection said they had to go.

The next stage to McCue turning his dream into reality occurred in the spring of 1910. Late in March he and two other men traveled to Colby, Oakley, and Russell Springs to meet with local citizens. The purpose of the trip was probably to gauge support for constructing a railroad north from Scott City. Without a doubt there was a great deal of interest in Russell Springs.

Since its creation in the 1880's Russell Springs had been the seat of Logan County. Its growth was hampered by the fact that no railroad had built through the community. The prospect of McCue's line gave hope to the town that it might have a future after all. Because this was so important to Russell Springs, it's not surprising that its newspaper, the *Leader*, would not only trumpet the project but be the main source for news about it over the next year.

Scott City was also interested in the project, although on June 17 the *News Chronicle* reported that it would be extended south to Liberal, not north. But a few weeks later grading of the line to the north was underway. The route would start at Scott City, run north-northwest to Russell Springs, then northwest to Winona on the Union Pacific. In Russell Springs a committee was formed to encourage people to buy railroad bonds and offer other support, a railroad meeting was held, and the Leader geared up its rhetoric.

On July 8 under the headline "Don't Knock--Boost," the *Leader* proclaimed that most of the community supported the railroad project. "If any reader has been inclined to join the knockers we say don't!" it urged. The promoters might not make any money with the railroad, and the newspaper didn't think it was important if they did. The tracks were vital to the community, it implied, and if anything did go wrong only those truly on board would have any right to complain.

Despite this some opposition surfaced to the new Scott City & Northern railroad. In the fall a petition was presented to the Logan County commission to resubmit a railroad bond proposition to county voters. The commissioners refused to accept the petition and put the matter to the ballot. The reason for the petition seems murky, but may have been a combination of actual opposition to the railroad and local interests with ties to Gove County.

The latter reason was due in part to the fact that the county seat, the town of Gove, also didn't have a railroad. In November the *News Chronicle* was reporting that the SCN route was changing northeast to enter Gove. Russell Springs was crushed and Gove was ecstatic about the shift. Then in January of 1911 it was announced that bond elections would be held across Logan County that month. What's more, the road's surveyors were staking out the line through Russell Springs and the grading crews were halfway between there and Scott City.

Late in January the bond issues passed largely by wide margins in the five Logan County townships where the line was projected. There was still opposition to the bonds in Beaver Township in Scott County, but it couldn't stop the progress of the SCN. Work continued through the winter, not even stopping when an explosion accident injured a worker (he had some burns and bruises but nothing was broken).

Various rumors floated about the SCN as construction continued. McCue was in talks to sell the GCG&N to the Santa Fe. In March SCN officials met with men from the UP, perhaps with the goal of selling this line to them. Nothing came of it, nor of the word that Russell Springs would get the railroad's main facilities.

More important was that in May the town of Russell Springs voted against giving city support to the SCN by one vote. An accusation of irregularity surfaced in how the vote was held, but the setback didn't stop work. Around the middle of June the tracks reached Russell Springs. There was no stopping to celebrate, however; the road had to be completed to Winona by July 4 to obtain the bonds voted there.

The crews raced to lay track and with an hour to spare finished the Scott City Northern into Winona, completing a route just over 50 miles long. The track was a bit rough on the section from Russell Springs to Winona, but the railroad was done. A grand celebration was held in Winona and attended by people from around the area. Scott City and Winona teams won baseball games, and festivities concluded with a dance and a play.

The first SCN passenger train schedules appeared in local newspapers in late July. Train No. 1 left Winona at 7:00 AM, reached Russell Springs half an hour later, and arrived in Scott City at 9:30. Train No. 2 left Scott City at 2:00 PM and arrived in Winona at 4:30. The equipment of the SCN consisted of three locomotives, three passenger cars, and 15 freight or baggage cars. The main source of traffic were the farms and villages along the route. An account published years later stated that because the SCN didn't get much business, train crewmen could run errands for passengers at a village stop!

Throughout the rest of 1911 and into 1912 not much else happened to the railroad. At the end of 1912 the railroad announced a new timetable. No. 1 would leave Winona at 1:30 PM and arrived in Scott City at 4:30; No. 2 would leave Scott City at 9:45 AM and reach Winona three hours later. Each way the time between Winona and Russell Springs was increased to about 45 minutes. This could suggest more business, but most likely it meant that the trains were running slower due to deferred maintenance. The following year would see more problems for the railroad.

1913 began well enough for the SCN. In January a story emerged in the *Scott County Republican* that the road would be purchased by the Missouri, Kansas & Texas railroad. The MK&T, or "Katy," was interested in securing a line from the Gulf of Mexico to Denver. Portions of the route from Oklahoma south were already in the Katy's hands. The Katy would secure both the SCN and the GCG&N, at that point operated by the Santa Fe, and would then build a line from Garden City to Forgan, Oklahoma. From Winona the Katy hoped to secure trackage rights on the UP to enter Colorado's capital. A month later the *News Chronicle* reported SCN surveyors were looking at a route to Goodland for a similar purpose. By May the story had changed to suggest that the Midland Valley, running from Wichita to Fort Smith, Arkansas, was interested in the SCN for a Denver line.

The Scott City Northern

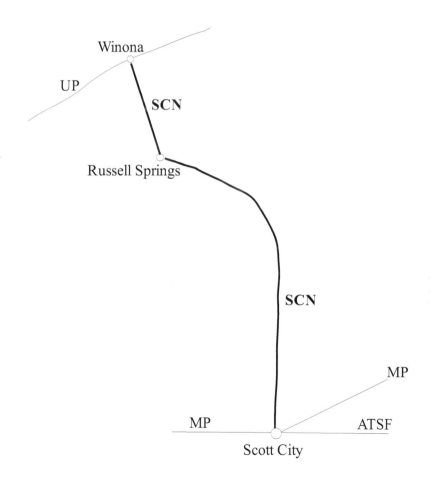

point operated by the Santa Fe, and would then build a line from Garden City to Forgan, Oklahoma. From Winona the Katy hoped to secure trackage rights on the UP to enter Colorado's capital. A month later the *News Chronicle* reported SCN surveyors were looking at a route to Goodland for a similar purpose. By May the story had changed to suggest that the Midland Valley, running from Wichita to Fort Smith, Arkansas, was interested in the SCN for a Denver line.

But by now the SCN was in real trouble. In April the Commonwealth Trust Company of St. Louis, apparently a major investor in the road, sued to foreclose on the Scott City Northern. The reason for the suit seems to be that B. A. McCue put himself into debt to finish the SCN. He wasn't able to pay what he owed to the trust company, and they sued to recover their loss. The railroad was sold at a sheriff's auction on August 6 to the Colorado, Kansas & Oklahoma Company. The line would be operated under the CK&O name, but the schedule remained the same and talks continued with the Katy.

Sadly these talks never when anywhere and the railroad continued to struggle. But there could have been important political and social ramifications if the north-south effort had succeeded. A completed railroad would have tied several western Kansas communities and counties together. This could then have been a springboard to them joining to achieve other common goals. Instead of the high plains looking east for support and inspiration, these communities might have been able to look to each other.

The CK&O soldiered on for the next few years, operating a single mixed train (a freight train with a passenger car or two at the end) each way every day except Sundays. Things started to happen again late in 1916 when calls were renewed from southwestern Kansas for a connection between the CK&O and the MK&T. Citizens from Cimarron began lobbying railroad officials in November, and further meetings were held in Liberal in January.

The communities along the line were supportive of the new effort. The January 3, 1917, issue of the *News Chronicle* reported that over a fourth of Scott County's tax base came from railroad taxes. The Missouri Pacific paid the most in 1916, the Santa Fe was second, and the CK&O paid just under $860. The newspaper speculated that should the CK&O extension be built, the railroad would be bumped up to a "through road." This would boost the taxes it paid to around $30,000. Since this amount was a third more than the taxes paid by the MP and the Santa Fe combined, it seems on the face of it to be questionable. But county revenues would go up if the extension went into operation, and that was one more argument in its favor.

As 1917 began it seemed that the old extension of the MK&T might finally become a reality. The lawsuit between B. A. McCue and his St. Louis creditor ended in February. In March Finney County voted in favor of bonds for construction of the line, and local man Ben Allen was promoted to CK&O treasurer and superintendent. Over the summer survey crews began to lay out the route of the extension south from Garden City. The Kansas body regulating public utilities, including railroads, approved a CK&O proposal to issue stock and bonds at the end of July.

But just one month later things began to shift. In August the railroad asked the Public Utilities Commission for permission to abandon the segment from Russell Springs to Winona. The stated reason was to built a smoother line to the Union Pacific along the Smoky Hill River to McAllaster. Winona quickly mobilized to protest the abandonment, and in late September the request was withdrawn.

Then on October 1, 1917, railroad officials dropped a bombshell: the Federal court in Leavenworth was about to order the discontinuance of the CK&O.

A meeting was held in Russell Springs to organize a fight to save the railroad. People from all along the line turned out, angry that the money they had put forward to obtain the railroad was about to be lost. They believed firmly that if the railroad was properly managed it could succeed. The county attorneys of Logan and Scott Counties raced to Topeka to confer with the state attorney general. They were also encouraged to go before the Commission to protest the abandonment.

The efforts to save the CK&O seemed to pay off when a week later the Federal judge granted a stay. The road's supporters were to be given 90 days to prove their assertion that if run well the railroad could turn a profit. Local citizens would have to put up money to purchase the railroad and its equipment. The supporters were further encouraged by a statement by the Commission's chairman opposing the abandonment, and by word that the Garden City Sugar Company was willing to buy the CK&O and operate it.

The effort led in mid-October to a first in Kansas railroad history. Judge John Pollock issued a ruling that would allow the two counties along the CK&O to buy and run the railroad. This decision preceded by several decades the creation of the Mid-States Port Authority to take over a former Rock Island line, and of efforts in recent years by other Kansas communities to preserve short lines.

The price for the CK&O as stated by Judge Pollock was $250,000. To begin the process the judge stipulated that Scott and Logan County had to put up a $20,000 bond. Fundraising began immediately, and it seems that by the end of the month the initial money was raised. But because it wasn't in cash or bank notes the Judge refused to accept it.

The supporters turned in early November to Otto Byers, owner of the Anthony & Northern railroad. They engaged Byers into talking to a potential guarantor in Wichita. Byers encouraged the people to "exhaust every effort" to save the CK&O. Byers had his own interest as well, as his son owned land along the proposed extension.

The effort was not enough, however, and the court appointed a prominent man from Cowley County, W. P. Hackney, as Special Master. In mid-November Hackney announced that the CK&O would be put up for sale at an auction on December 15, 1917. The auction went on as planned and a Chicago firm bought the line for its scrap value. The United States had entered World War One earlier in the year, and the road's equipment and rails were needed elsewhere.

But the supporters had one last hope. America's entry into the war also meant that the Federal government had to take over the nation's railroads to assure that its war priorities would be met. The CK&O's boosters got in touch with one of the state's two Senators, Charles Curtis. Senator Curtis persuaded Federal authorities to examine the railroad for the possibility of a takeover. The hope was that the takeover would give the supporters time to raise money to buy the line. They were disappointed when in late January the government declined to take over the CK&O. Soon after the railroad was scrapped.

The community hit hardest by the loss of the railroad was Russell Springs. Without it the town lost any chance of attracting new businesses, especially an industry that could have provided jobs over the long term. The population declined steadily. An effort began to move the county seat to Oakley in the 1930's. The effort succeeded in the mid-1960s, and by the end of the 20th Century Russell Springs had an official population of only 29.

The SCN-CK&O had a chance to be more than just a minor short-line railroad in western Kansas. It could have joined a region, brought jobs and revenue to the communities it connected, and prevented a town from losing the county seat. But its failure once again shows how important it is for communities to work together for their mutual benefit.

SABOTAGED BY FATE & GREED:
THE TRANSCONTINENTAL CHANCE OF THE U.P.E.D.

The Kansas Pacific railroad is best known as the shipper of the cattle driven from Texas to Abilene, Kansas, during the glory days of the Chisholm Trail. A fact not quite as known but more important is that it was the first railroad to build across Kansas and thus the first to enter Denver from the east. Only the last push of the line, from extreme western Kansas into Colorado was built under the "Kansas Pacific" name. Mush of the line was constructed when the railroad was called the "Union Pacific, Eastern Division."

When that name was given to the company in 1863 its backers had high hopes that the UPED might be able to outflank its rival and build "the" transcontinental railroad. These hopes were not without foundation. The UPED laid its first rail before its rival the Union Pacific. The UPED was supported by powerful men in Kansas and in Washington. But when the first transcontinental line was completed in 1869, it was the UP that had finished the eastern section. The UPED was still struggling to get the capital to complete construction to Denver.

The reason why the UPED failed to reach its lofty goal hinges on events that took place over four crucial years. The actions of backers of the road from 1862 to 1865 would end up undermining the dreams of the UPED. That story involves stock giveaways, white knights, internecine warfare, and even a cold-blooded murder on the streets of a Kansas town.

That story begins in the early days of the troubled Kansas Territory. In August of 1855 the pro-slavery territorial legislature created the Leavenworth, Pawnee & Western railroad company. The LP&W was to build a railroad from the territory's main city at the time, Leavenworth, west along the Kansas River to the area of Fort Riley. From there the railroad was to follow the Smoky Hill River to the 100th meridian. The LP&W was allowed to issue some $5 million in stock and ordered to begin construction by 1860.

For the next two years nothing happened with the project. Then in late 1856 some of the pro-slavery backers of the railroad began to worry about the fate of the LP&W. The abolitionist forces were gaining control of the territory. When they did they might be inclined to harm the interests of the LP&W. Therefore the backers decided to bring in free-state men to help the road's prospects. The men that joined the company were Hugh Ewing and his brother, Thomas Ewing, Jr.

Thomas Ewing, Jr., had only been in the territory a year, but already he had a shine on his name. He was the son of an Ohio Senator and cabinet member; former personal secretary to President Zachary Taylor; a cousin of James G. Blaine; and brother-in-law of William T. Sherman. Once he had come to Kansas he became one of the founders of the Republican Party. Within two years of his entry into the LP&W Ewing would be elected chief justice of the state supreme court.

When Ewing came on board he was put on the road's board of directors while his brother Hugh was elected president. The company began offering stock and in May of 1857 it hired a surveyor to map out a route. Soon the LP&W ran into its first obstructions in the form of two Indian reservations, the Delawares east of Lawrence and the Pottawatomies west of Topeka.

The road's promoters realized that these reservations could be a boon to the company if they could make a deal. If the LP&W could acquire the land, it could use the sales of that land as income to pay for construction. Ownership of the land could be used as collateral for loans. And any land that wasn't sold before the rails were laid was certain to increase in value. An effort led by Ewing began to obtain land from those tribes by any means necessary.

The attempt was at first directed at getting land grants from the federal government. This led nowhere for the next three years because of the rising national conflict over slavery. The political struggle over Kansas' admission to the Union also stalled the lobbying for land grants. Then in 1860 the leaders of the LP&W had an idea: why not negotiate directly with the two tribes?

This is exactly what they did. First they put together a treaty with the Delaware that would allow the LP&W to buy any land on their reservation that was not surveyed and assigned to members of the tribe. To suppress any opposition from within and without the treaty donated land for churches and schools, and gave Delaware chiefs $1,500 a year from any money the railroad paid to the federal government. Ewing and his friends worked quietly, and with little or no fanfare their treaty became law on August 27, 1860.

Once that work was done Ewing used his influence to get prominent Kansans to support the LP&W. He also employed his connections to overcome opposition to the treaty from whites and unsatisfied Delawares. Ewing was even able to gain the support of the new President, Abraham Lincoln. By the fall of 1861 the treaty had been modified enough to squelch dissent. The road's backers now turned to the Pottawatomies.

Again Ewing and his friends negotiated directly with the tribe and again they were able to secure a treaty. But now Ewing had to work harder to gain political support. One of the state's new Senators, Samuel Pomeroy, was from Atchison and had his own "pet railroad." In order to get Pomeroy's backing Ewing had to hand out LP&W stock. The other Senator, James Lane, not only wanted stock for him and his friends but also demanded that his chief rival in Kansas politics, Governor Charles Robinson, be ousted from the board of directors. Ewing needed Lane's help if the treaties were to be passed, so he complied with Lane's terms.

With the treaties safely ensconced into law Ewing turned his attention to impending legislation on a transcontinental railroad. In the 1850's national efforts to create such a project were stalled by sectional conflict. With the exit of the southern states and the start of the Civil War, prospects for the legislation soared. Ewing and his allies were determined that the LP&W would take some part in that enterprise.

An intense lobbying campaign got underway in the spring of 1862 to insure a place for the railroad in the Pacific Railway Act. The campaign was fairly successful; when the Act was passed the LP&W was to be given subsidies, chances for government loans, and formal status of its route to the 100th meridian. But it was unable to get the power to determine where the official transcontinental company, the Union Pacific, would start its construction.

This, enhanced by Ewing's stock handouts, were two of the main obstacles to the transcontinental dream of the railroad. The UP would be able to chart its own course without hindrance from the Kansas road's backers. The stock handouts left confusion as to the control of the company. That in turn led to a series of lawsuits that plagued the railroad throughout the 1860's. These suits made it difficult for the company to obtain capital from easterners while the UP had no trouble raising funds.

At the time the Pacific Railway Act was passed Ewing seemed to lose interest in the railroad. He also took a greater interest in the prospects of a political career. To that end he enlisted in the Union Army. He was unable to aid the LP&W further, and in 1863 he left the company altogether.

That year two men took control of the company. Their actions are the next part of the story. The men were John C. Fremont and Samuel Hallett. They bought controlling interest in company stock on May 28, 1863. They quickly reorganized the company and renamed it the Union Pacific, Eastern Division.

Fremont was of course the more famous of the two new leaders of the railroad. He had gained fame as a western explorer in the 1840's. He enhanced that fame by running as the first Republican candidate for President in 1856. In 1861 he took command of Union forces in Missouri. He tried to enforce harsh policies on Missouri slave-owners, which endangered Missouri's status as a Union state. In the field he was unable to engage Confederate forces, which angered radicals in Kansas. He came to the railroad a man on a downward path to obscurity.

Samuel Hallett, however, was a rising star in railroad circles. He was a young New York investment banker. He was a financial agent for the successful Atlantic & Great Western railroad. He had strong connections with businessmen and investors both in American and in Europe. Hallett quickly became the UPED's driving force.

The first action Hallett took was to dismiss the contractors Ewing's group had hired. At the same time he leaked a letter from John Usher, a one-time railroad supporter now serving as Secretary of the Interior, that said the administration favored the Kansas River route for the transcontinental project. Hallett then requested that Leavenworth take $100,000 in railroad stock.

Leavenworth balked at Hallett's demand. Part of the reason was that they were busy aiding Lawrence, which was nearly destroyed in the horrific Quantrill raid. Another reason may have been that Hallett could see Leavenworth wasn't getting their act together about backing railroads. Political infighting prevented city leaders from uniting behind the UPED or anything else. The community was also unwilling to "share" a railroad with other cities. One nearby newspaper editor wrote on that score that Leavenworth would run "their" railroad "into the ground for fear of having it go to some other town."

Hallett got back at recalcitrant Leavenworth by moving the

company's offices to Wyandotte (part of present-day Kansas City, Kansas). This would align the UPED with Kansas City, Missouri. Although only a village compared with Leavenworth, Kansas City had both the unity and the will to cooperate that the other city lacked. Its leaders were already behind one project to center a Great Lakes-Gulf of Mexico on their community. They quickly got behind Hallett and the UPED.

In December of 1863 ground was finally broken on the "Omaha road." On the UPED, the line had been graded from Wyandotte to Lawrence and the first rails arrived. More rail arrived in February along with the road's first locomotive, the Wyandotte. Another locomotive went into service in March, and by mid-April ten miles of track were in service.

Hallett had wanted to bypass Lawrence and Topeka because both towns sat south of the Kansas River. Hallett was strong-armed by Senator Lane into building to both towns. Despite this dispute, the struggle to find laborers, and the problem of acquiring iron and locomotives in the middle of the Civil War, the UPED was moving west at a steady pace.

Then in April Hallett and Fremont had a falling out. The cause seems to have stemmed from an alliance Fremont and his friends had with a UPED stockholder who was also a director of the UP. Hallett managed to drive out Fremont and his supporters, but in doing so he further harmed the road's chances of building part of the transcontinental railroad. He had brought in a group led by John D. Perry, a St. Louis banker. Perry seemed to have been more interested in making money from a railroad than in running one. This would be no problem so long as Hallett stayed in control of the project.

Then came the hard hand of fate, in the form of Orlando Talcott.

Talcott had worked for the UPED and was one of Fremont's men. When he was fired after Fremont's ouster he sent a critical report to Washington about the railroad. Hallett found out about the report, and he ordered one of his brothers to slap Talcott the next time he saw him. He did so, and Talcott decided to get revenge.

On the afternoon of July 27, 1864, as Hallett was walking to the road's office in Wyandotte, he was shot in the back by Talcott. Hallett turned, saw Talcott, and said "My God! he has shot me." He repeated this several times, sank to the ground, groaned once, gasped once, and then died on the street.

Talcott promised to surrender himself to passersby. But while they went to help Hallett, Talcott mounted his horse and rode away to Quindaro (also now part of Kansas City, Kansas). Once in Quindaro he promised again to surrender himself when caught by a local law enforcement officer. He asked the officer to speak to a lawyer first, and used that opportunity to escape.

Hallett's death was the most significant factor in the failure of the UPED to become a transcontinental railroad. He was energetic and dedicated to the railroad. When he was murdered he was about to open the first 40 miles of track. He could have easily pushed the road west quickly. The UPED could have reached the 100th meridian before the UP, which did so in 1866.

Hallett might have also been able to finesse the problems the road encountered later. Although Hallett was strong-willed he was also smart. He had been able to reach an accommodation with Lane over crossing the river to enter Lawrence and Topeka. He might have been able to negotiate with the federal government when it started to turn against the UPED and towards the UP. He might also have been able to persuade investors in putting their capital into the road despite any trouble it ran into.

As it was, after Hallett's death Perry managed to oust Hallett's brothers from the UPED and to some degree swindle his widow out of her inheritance. This again tied the railroad up in litigation. While this went on Usher left the Interior and was replaced by James Harlan, an Iowan who backed the UP. These developments would allow the UP to overtake its Kansas rival in the race west.

The UPED continued building towards the Rocky Mountains. In December of 1864 the road was opened to Lawrence. It reached Topeka a year later; Junction City at the end of 1866; was in Hays in October of 1867; and was within 40 miles of the Colorado border by September of 1868. Construction halted for a year, then resumed under the leadership of William J. Palmer.

As part of the new Kansas Pacific, Palmer took an interest in extending the road to the Pacific Ocean. After reaching Denver in August of 1870 the KP started up the Arkansas Valley Railway. This line was to build from the main at Kit Carson, Colorado, towards Las Animas with the idea of continuing on into New Mexico. Only the section from Carson to Animas was built. The line never made money, and the Atchison, Topeka & Santa Fe rapidly pushed through southeastern Colorado to Santa Fe. Palmer saw that the KP was no longer interested in building further west, and he left to start up the

Denver & Rio Grande Railway.

The transcontinental dream of the LP&W-UPED-KP was over.

It's unlikely that the history of the West would have been radically different had the Kansas road beaten the UP in the race to the Pacific. There was of course more than one transcontinental line constructed. White settlement would still have driven out the Indians, there would still have been cattle drives and cowtowns, and the urban centers of the modern West would have still sprung up. The one thing that would have been different is that the Kansas Pacific might be what the Union Pacific is now. A longshot, perhaps, but history is littered with longshots that made it. The Kansas road could have been one of those successful longshots.

"ANOTHER TERRIBLE MASSACRE":
THE STORY BEHIND THE VICTORIA RAILROAD CEMETERY

Drive east of Hays, Kansas, on old highway US-40 about ten miles to the outskirts of Victoria. Along the south side of the road, near the railroad bridge over Cathedral Street, are six graves marked with small stones. A large granite marker with an old plaque and a modern flagpole makes this site more visible to traffic. This site is known locally as the Victoria Railroad Cemetery.

Next to many highways and county roads across the West are similar burial sites. The vast majority of these sites are pioneer cemeteries. Those interred usually belonged to a single family that homesteaded near the graves. What makes the Victoria site unique is that the men laid to rest here were not pioneers but railroad workers buried close to where they were killed.

The men died in an Indian attack during the summer of 1867. They worked for the Union Pacific Eastern Division. The became victims of the struggle to bring American civilization to the West, and the resistance to that struggle by the native inhabitants of the Great Plains. Were it not for their special "cemetery," their tragedy might have been forgotten among a litany of violence in that terrible year.

The UPED once had hopes of surpassing the Union Pacific as the nation's westbound transcontinental railroad. By January of 1867 that dream had died. The railroad was now working to be the first to cross the state, and perhaps lay the first track into Denver.

As the year began prospects looked good. The end of the track was at the eastern border of Dickinson County. A survey party had plotted the route as far west as Fort Hays. Construction had halted during the winter, but resumed in March.

On March 14 the tracks reached new town of Abilene in Dickinson County, already planning for cattle drives up from Texas. A flood slowed construction so that Salina, the seat of Saline County and immediately to the west of Dickinson, wasn't reached until April 20. By the end of May track crews were past Fort Harker, near present-day Kanopolis in Ellsworth County.

Now the UPED was entering the domain of the Plains tribes.

There were concerns about Indian attacks, but no one imagined the scale of the assaults.

On May 18 a survey party was attacked near Monument Station (now in Logan County). More attacks came in June in Ellsworth County and near Bunker Hill (Russell County). The situation was critical because the crews were largely unarmed, and far from the Army forts of northern Kansas. As the attacks continued and casualties among the crews increased, the railroad's president wired Governor Samuel Crawford for help. Guns and ammunition were sent to the UPED's employees.

Calls to the generals in command of Army troops in Kansas went unheeded. Because of this on July 1, 1867, Governor Samuel Crawford began raising eight companies of volunteer cavalry. Known as the Eighteenth Kansas Volunteer Regiment, the soldiers were to go into the field and bring the raiding tribes to heel.

By the end of the month Kansas newspapers were filled with accounts of Indian deprivations. One story that made the rounds was of G.S. Cook, a freighter employed by the government, who fought a few hundred Arapahoe, Cheyenne, and Sioux warriors at the small Army post at Monument Station. Other accounts told of a party attacked near Fort Hays; of men and women fleeing the area; and even a locomotive being moved for fear of capture. The Junction City Union claimed that the strength of all the tribes "engaged in hostilities" throughout the west was 78,000.

An anonymous writer from Fort Wallace, the westernmost of the Kansas forts, sent a letter to the *Leavenworth Daily Conservative* about the situation. Published on August 6, the author claimed that half of the attacks on whites weren't being reported. He dismissed as absurd claims of "Eastern newspapers" that the trouble was being blown out of proportion "to involve the Government in debt." His belief was that the Army was being outwitted and outfought. He concluded by dismissing proposals of the formation of a peace commission, saying that "they will only succeed in spending the $450,000, and in prolonging the trouble."

It was in this climate of fear that the massacre of August 1 took place.

It took anywhere from a week to ten days for news from Fort Hays to reach the major newspapers of eastern Kansas. The first account appeared in Leavenworth *Conservative* as early as August 4. The report, posted from Fort Harker, stated that seven workers of a grading party had been killed near Fort Hays. A later dispatch confirmed the deaths, and added that horses were also stolen from nearby Big Creek Station.

The next accounts appeared on August 6 in the *Kansas Daily Tribune* of Lawrence and the *Leavenworth Times*. The *Emporia News* reported the incident on August 9. The *Tribune* and the *Conservative* added details to earlier stories on August 11. The longest story published was in the *Leavenworth Daily Commercial* of August 10. From these sources we can piece together what happened to the seven men about ten miles east of Fort Hays.

The men appear to have been taken by surprise while hard at work. What they were doing remains unclear; perhaps they were a survey party or advance grading crew. Two to three dozen Cheyenne warriors attacked the seven railroad men. The men were either unarmed or had their guns out of easy reach. At least five of the seven were killed outright. Most of the news accounts agreed that two of the five were scalped. The *Times* claimed one of scalped men lived, and was taken to the Fort where he died. The *Commercial* said that one was found alive but died just before reaching Fort.

After the first attack the Cheyennes tried to ambush another group of workers Farther east. Those men were armed and fended off the Cheyenne attack. The warriors then moved to Big Creek Station, a stage station several miles southeast of the Fort. They stole a number of horses and mules before retreating under fire from stage employees and soldiers.

The names of the seven killed varied from paper to paper. Incredibly, the *Tribune* listed eight names: P. S. Ashley, Foreman Broadhead, Thomas Curry, Charles Watson, Joseph Harrington, Patrick Rafferty, Hugh McDonegle, and William Gould. It also said that the "first six" were buried on site, while Gould was buried at Fort. The *Conservative* listed the names as P. S. Ashley, who was the foreman of the group, a man named only as "Broadhead," Charles Watson, Thomas Carney, Pat Rafferty, John Harrington, and a "McDonough." The *Times* printed the names P. S. "Ashby," Thomas Coney, Charles Watson, John Harrington, Pat Rafferty, Hugh McDonough, and William Gould. The only name carved on one of the stone markers is that of "Henry McDonney."

There was an equal amount of confusion about where these men were from. The *Times* mentioned the places origin of three: Coney and Watson were from Iowa, while Harrington was from St. Louis. The *Conservative* reported that Broadhead was from Wisconsin; Watson, from Canada; Carney, Iowa; Rafferty, Kansas City; Harrington, St. Louis; and McDonough, Boston. The *Tribune* stated that Ashley and Broadhead were from Wisconsin; agreed with the Conservative about "Curry" (Carney), Harrington, and Rafferty; said "McDonegle" was from Denver City; and that Gould was from Illinois.

All this confusion between accounts could be explained by the inaccuracy of reporting in those days, and possibly conflicted telegraph messages from various individuals. There may also be another explanation, gleaned from an article by Otto Byers. Byers came to work for the railroad in 1878, at the start of a career that would eventually see him become president of a railroad in central Kansas.

Although Byers came to the road over a decade after these events, he may have known veteran employees who were at work during the late 1860's. In the article he wrote about the railroad in the late 1920's he stated that many railroad's employees at the time were "little less than desperadoes." He added that often men did not work under their true names, and that personal questions were violently resented.

If there was confusion about who had died, there was less about what should be done. At least three Kansas newspapers took the opportunity to complain about the situation in western Kansas and offer solutions. The weekly Topeka Tribune, while it didn't report on the attack, did reprint a nearly vicious editorial from the St. Louis Democrat that called for reservations and extermination as punishment.

Under the headline "More Indian Murders," the Leavenworth *Times* offered a more mellow commentary on the impact of the story:

> "We have just had another terrible massacre," says the report.
> "Another -- that strange, awful and in a savage land a fearful word, -- another, and yet another will follow, too, unless Government shall act with resolved will, and as a unit."

The *Commercial* was more harsh, but directed its hostility at the government:

"Thus another massacre goes unpunished, simply because the American nation, with a large army and department commanders drawing an immense salary, has not sufficient troops at any one post to chastise a band of thieving Indians. The savages in almost every engagement laugh at and insult our troops, gathering like bees around the pitiful handful of men that the commanders of our posts have at their disposal.

"The total number of Indians on the war path is about three thousand, while we have almost as many Indian Commissioners and Major Generals. Truly, there is something rotten in Denmark."

The soldiers and officers posted at Fort Hays were aware within hours of the massacre that had occurred to the east. Around two o'clock on the afternoon of August 1 word arrived at the Fort. History doesn't record how the Fort gained knowledge of the situation or who alerted them. It's likely that one or more members of the second group of UPED workers attacked in the raid reported the massacre to the Fort.

Fort Hays in the late summer 1867 was still under construction. The first Army post in the area was established in October 1865 as Fort Fletcher. Located several miles east-southeast at the junction of Big Creek and its North Fork, Fletcher was garrisoned for less than a year before lack of funds closed it. Troops moved back late in 1866, moved the post north slightly, and the name was changed to Fort Hays. The new site flooded in early June 1867, so the Fort was moved to its final site later that month. The soldiers stationed here were still living in tents, waiting for stone buildings to be completed, when news of the massacre reached them.

Elements of three regiments were on hand to deal with the situation. The Seventh Cavalry had been at the Fort since its move. The post commander had asked for more troops, and a company of the Thirty-Eighth Infantry and Company F of the Tenth Cavalry were sent. These latter two were units composed of black soldiers.

Company F, under the command of Captain George Armes, was sent to scene of the day's attacks. Armes found the Indian trail, determined that there were more than he could deal with, and sent for reinforcements. He hoped to be joined by men from the Thirty-Eighth and a cannon. When they failed to arrive on the morning of August 2, Armes decided to give pursuit.

He had started out from Fort Hays with 44 men. He had sent six back to get assistance. Four men became sick, probably from the same cholera outbreak that was ravaging the Kansas plains at the time. Armes went after the Indians with 34 men, including two white scouts.

The force moved fifteen miles north to the Saline River. After marching another 12 miles along the river the force was attacked by 75 Indian warriors. Within minutes Armes command was surrounded. He pushed out by moving his men towards the Fort, but then became surrounded again by even more warriors. The Indians appeared to have kept their distance, with only an occasional warrior riding through Armes' position.

One of his sergeants was killed in the fight, while his first sergeant and two corporals had their horses shot from under them. Armes himself was wounded in the hip. Some of his men panicked at that point, but his Lieutenant and the two scouts were able to keep the rest disciplined.

The Indians did fire intensely into the command. Armes believed they were unable to inflict more casualties was due having new guns that they had not gotten used to. It may also have been that the warriors hoped to panic the whole force before closing in.

Armes noticed that there were two whites with the Indians. Various accounts suggest that the whites, either half-breeds or fully white, were either leading the attack or playing a significant role. Armes directed some of his fire at the two, but with no effect. He believed that during the engagement he had killed six and wounded several more, out of a total force of 350 to 400.

Armes was able to extricate his company from the battlefield and return to Fort Hays on August 3. His reinforcements had tried to reach him, but he had left before they did so. That force marched up the North Fork of Big Creek, then to the Saline where they ran into fifty Indians. They fired three shells at the Indians who promptly scattered.

This battle was the first time that the black cavalry troopers of either the Ninth or the Tenth had seen combat on the plains. Sergeant William Christy, a farmer from Pennsylvania who had enlisted a day under two months before, was the first combat death of both regiments. Company F of the Tenth were no longer recruits; they were veterans. Not long after this action these troopers would earn their famous nickname, "buffalo soldiers."

As word spread around the area of the massacre of the seven, other

UPED construction workers raced to Fort Hays for protection. But instead of keeping out of trouble the workers got into trouble.

Hays City was springing up between the Fort and the railroad right-of-way. Already saloons were opening and whiskey was flowing. The workers promptly got drunk and demoralized. Soldiers were dispatched to escort the workers back to their camps. Whiskey peddlers spread rumors of more danger, the workers returned, and again they had to be escorted back to their camps.

Despite his wounds Captain Armes went back on duty. His first charge was to restore morale among the construction crews. Other attacks occurred west of the Fort, so Armes and his troopers were dispatched to stop them. Late in August elements of the Tenth and the Eighteenth Kansas fought another large Indian force in an action known as the battle of Beaver Creek.

This is the Victoria Railroad Cemetery, as photographed in 2003. The granite marker is to the left of the flagpole; the carved stone is under glass to the right of the flagpole. The pole flies an American flag and a Union Pacific flag in this picture. The metal fencing is new. *Author's photo.*

Indian raids on the UPED continued into September. A peace council was finally held in October at Medicine Lodge Creek. In exchange for hunting rights and annuities, the tribes present agreed to give up any further claims to the land north of the Arkansas River. The Medicine Lodge Treaty held for a time, but it would take another year and an even more bitter campaign to bring peace to the central plains.

The tracks of the Union Pacific Eastern Division reached the Fort Hays area that same October. An effort to establish a town along the line called Rome had failed due to cholera and lack of railroad support. The depot was put in at Hays City, and Hays City thrived.

Construction resumed in 1868, and by September was close to Fort Wallace. Work halted for two years while railroad backers searched for more capital. With new funding the work resumed in 1870. Track was laid at a furious pace, with the line completed to Denver on August 15, 1870. By then the company had taken over the Denver & Pacific, which had built from that city to Cheyenne, Wyoming, on the line of the Union Pacific.

The railroad's name had also changed in 1870 to "Kansas Pacific." The KP had become prosperous thanks to the cattle trade. In 1867 the cattle drives from Texas to Abilene had begun. They were more successful than anyone had predicted. The KP did well with the steady stream of cattle traffic it carried during the summer and fall.

Things began to go wrong for the KP in 1872. Abilene had become a rough town thanks to the cattle drives. A marshal had tamed the tough elements in 1870 and another in 1871, but the community grew tired of the effort. After the 1871 drives ended Abilene sent word to Texas that they didn't want any more.

Meanwhile the Atchison, Topeka & Santa Fe railroad had built its own line across the state. Its route was well to the south of the KP, making it a closer shipping line. The drives now terminated at Santa Fe towns, first at Newton for a year, then Wichita, then Dodge City.

The KP struggled on through the rest of the 1870's. Late in the decade in became a pawn in the feud between railroad speculator Jay Gould and the owners of the Union Pacific. Gould tried to compel the UP to take over the KP, but its owners refused to play his game. Gould then assembled a system that included the KP and other railroads. His system would allow traffic to be moved from Cheyenne past Kansas City to St. Louis or points farther east. Faced with this considerable threat to their traffic, the UP had no choice but to take over the failing KP. In 1880 the Kansas Pacific ceased to exist, and its main route became the "Kansas Division" of the Union Pacific, which it has remained up to today.

Before the Kansas Pacific disappeared it made efforts to promote settlement along its line. Many small towns came into existence at that time, including one near the site of the 1867 massacre.

The town of Victoria was founded in 1873 by well-to-do Englishmen. They found it difficult to recreate their comfortable lifestyles on the Kansas prairie, and many gave up. Before they left they seem to have placed the first stones to mark the graves of the six railroad workers buried just south of the tracks.

One is carved to the memory of "Henry McDonney of Cambridge, Mass." This could be Hugh McDonegle, or McDonough, or his real name. Another says "Here lies -" while a third has only a cross carved onto it. A fourth, recently located and now under glass on a pedestal, has the most detail:

"Five persons here to me unknown, to their memory I've carved this stone, killed by Indians in ----- 1867, Dock Williams Carver"

The rest of the graves at this site are unmarked. There are a total of eleven graves here, more than can be accounted for by the attack in August of 1867. Later scholarship suggests that Victoria's founders may have used this site as their community cemetery before they left Kansas. Their departure did not lead to the end of Victoria. A new group of settlers followed, and under them the town thrived.

Many German Catholics were induced to settle southern Russia by Catherine the Great. One of the terms was that they would be exempt from military service. When in the 1870's the Czar decided to refuse to honor their exemption, these "Volga Germans" decided to emigrate to North America. Land agents of the KP encouraged them to settle around Hays. They created several new villages, and moved into both Hays and Victoria. In time they would build a grand church in Victoria known as the "Cathedral of Plains."

One man tried to bring attention to the deceased railroad workers and their grave site. James Behan came to Ellis County around 1877. He first made certain to copy down what was written on the small stones. Then around the turn of the century Behan persuaded the UP to erect a monument to mark the site. A large piece of granite was placed on a rock foundation and a plaque attached to the granite.

The exact date of the placing of this monument isn't known, but it may have been in late 1906. One thing that is known is that the plaque cites the wrong month for the date of the massacre, reading "October 1, 1867" instead of "August 1, 1867." The plaque does state that the site is the burial spot of six men, but doesn't say that seven were actually killed here.

Since there were no local newspapers to record the incident, it's clear that the story had been passed down orally. Errors had crept into the massacre narrative. These errors were repeated in the 1920's when the story of the Kansas Pacific briefly resurfaced.

Additional confusion arose over how many of the massacre victims were in fact buried. Stories surfaced that one of the corpses was removed and re-interred in his home state of Wisconsin. No dates have ever been given for this, so it's difficult to verify. However, this may also be due oral transmission of the story. One of the seven survived long enough to be carried to Fort Hays and was buried there. When the Army closed the Fort the bodies in its cemetery were moved, mainly to Fort Leavenworth. This might be the source of the account of the reburied victim.

When the Kansas Centennial occurred in 1961, and the Hays centennial six years later, most of the errors that had crept into the massacre story were corrected. The KP and the Victoria cemetery were given their due in books and articles that appeared through the late 1990's.

But that has not prevented the Victoria Railroad Cemetery from being bypassed by progress. Over three decades have passed since the last railroad passenger could look out his window at the site. Most cars race about a mile to the north along Interstate-70. What vehicles do use the former US-40 are likely just going between Hays and Victoria, never stopping to examine the grave site.

Few may now visit it, but that doesn't detract from its importance. There might be other similar places in Kansas and elsewhere, but this site continues to be open to the public and easily accessible. Ordinary people can stop, walk up to the graves, and reflect on the cost of opening the West.

This is the value of the Victoria Railroad Cemetery. This is why it, and the story behind it, should not be forgotten.

Robert Collins

THE MARION BELT & CHINGAWASSA SPRINGS: KANSAS' FIRST "EXCURSION" RAILROAD

Well before the first railroad began operation in Kansas, the novelty of the train had worn off. By then railroads were seen as a vital method of moving goods and people from place to place. Kansas towns wanted tracks laid through to bring settlers in and to ship agricultural and industrial products out. It's why an average-sized state like ours had so many railroad lines crisscrossing it.

In the last couple of decades there have been moves in various parts of the state to promote "railroad tourism." But railroad tourism is not a new idea. Many of Kansas' first railroads ran "excursion trains" to celebrate the laying of tracks to a new town or the completion of their line. Then there was the Marion Belt & Chingawassa Springs, a railroad whose main purpose was to run visitors to a resort and campground. Although the MB&CS didn't last very long, it nonetheless has a colorful and interesting story with (so far) a hopeful end.

The story begins with a mineral spring five miles northeast of Marion. The Kaw Indians appear to have known of the springs in the area for generations. Zebulon Pike may have been the first white man to become aware of them. A local legend grew up around one in particular that a chief named Chingawassa was murdered and buried there. Although there appears to have been an Osage chief with that name, there's no evidence that he was murdered or interred at Chingawassa Springs.

When white settlers founded the town of Marion they couldn't help noticing the nearby springs. Local residents occasionally camped there on holidays and during special events. But by 1888 notions of water cures and mineral springs resorts were sweeping the country. In June of that year the people of Marion invited university professors to examine Chingawassa Springs, probably with the idea of establishing just such a resort. Their report was very favorable towards the springs.

The only problem the town faced in exploiting Chingawassa's potential was transportation. The automobile and the bus were unknown. Wagons and stages would be too slow and could only carry so many. Clearly a railroad would have to be built to any resort at

Chingawassa if the project was to have any hope of attracting outsiders to it.

So in late January of 1889 the Marion Belt & Chingawassa Springs Railroad was created. The road was to have two routes. The first would start at the Marion Santa Fe depot, go east to a stone quarry, then northeast to the springs. The other route would go west from the depot along the south side of town to the Rock Island's tracks, then turn northwest to another group of quarries. The railroad would run passenger trains to the springs and resort, and freights to the quarries. Both the Santa Fe and the Rock Island were to cooperate with the MB&CS. The president of the new railroad would be New York banker John Hall. Levi Billings would be vice-president, C. S. Winslow secretary, and Samuel Howe treasurer. The railroad was granted a 99-year charter. It was capitalized with stock valued at $150,000.

The city of Marion would have to vote for a bond issue of $16,000 to get the first eight miles of the line built. However, the governor of the state had already cautioned towns against voting for any more bond issues. At least one resident of Marion, in the February 1 issue of the local newspaper the *Record*, picked up on the governor's message and urged careful consideration of the bond issue. But a week later Levi Billings wrote to *Record* readers that if there wasn't local support for the railroad nothing would happen.

This seemed to persuade the public, along with other hopes for additional industrial development along the line. The bonds carried on March 4 by a vote of 253 to 97. A few weeks later the city council passed an ordinance granting a right-of-way through Marion for the railroad, and by the end of the month surveyors were at work. The construction contract was let in April. Towards the end of the month the Record confidently predicted that the railroad would be finished by July 1.

For some reason the project slipped behind. This may have been due to delays at the springs themselves. By mid-July the railroad company had purchased additional land at the site. It built bridges and footpaths to the various springs, as well as a substantial structure that would serve as the depot and as a restaurant. Eventually there would be a hotel and a sanitarium at Chingawassa Springs as well.

On July 19 the *Record* announced that the tracks were finally laid. The formal opening would be on July 29, with plans for excursion trains to run through the summer and into the fall. Very little is now known about what equipment the MB&CS had for these trains. One former employee wrote in 1941 that the line had a "steam dummy engine, a 30 horse coal burner, and two passenger coaches." But there's no information from the period or after to indicate where the locomotive or the coaches came from. It's possible that the equipment came to the railroad used, and if so was likely from the Santa Fe or the Rock Island. The rails were said to be lighter than standard rails for the time. The line had no turntable to turn around the locomotive, just a passing siding, so it may have pulled the cars facing forward to the resort and pulled them facing backward to Marion.

The opening on July 29 appears to have been a success with visitors from all over the region coming in. Local families went out to see the site. Extra trains were running into Marion for some time. On August 13 editors from around the state were invited to see Chingawassa Springs. Many did so and wrote extravagantly, with an editor from Wellington calling Chingawassa "one of the wonders of Kansas" and one from Leoti saying that it was "destined to become the most famous summer resort and health sanitarium" in the state. Trains ran steadily every day until late that fall.

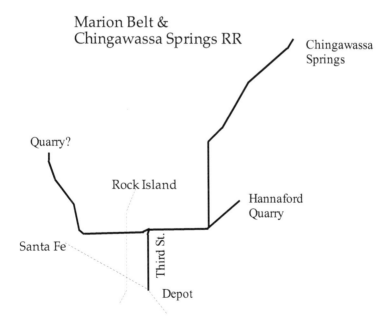

Marion Belt &
Chingawassa Springs RR

Chingawassa Springs

Quarry?

Rock Island

Hannaford Quarry

Santa Fe

Third St.

Depot

The baths at the resort reopened the next year on March 21. The following month the railroad was reorganized as the "Chingawassa Springs Railway Company." Around this time local citizens might have started to sour on the operation, but any nay-sayers were admonished by the *Record's* editor E. W. Hoch. The resort itself was formally opened for the 1890 season on June 5 with a local doctor setting up a practice there. On July 4 there were holiday celebrations at both the springs and in the town of Marion, which suggests that business was still strong.

The 1891 season at Chingawassa began around July 10, and the 1892 season on June 20. However, something may have happened between those years regarding the resort and the railroad. On January 29, 1892, *Record* editor E. W. Hoch published an article on the advantages of Marion County. Mention of the resort seems to have been minimal in the piece, and no mention of the railroad was given in a review of the county's rail network.

By this time there was a second newspaper being published in Marion, the *Times*. It began operation late in 1890, and as a result reported on the opening of the 1891 season on July 9. It also mentioned the name of the hotel at the springs, which was the Hotel El Dorado.

The *Times* appears to have taken the lead over the *Record* in promoting Chingawassa Springs in 1892. The first of its efforts came on June 23 with a front-page letter on the benefits of a visit to "Chingawasa Springs" by the doctor in charge of the resort, Dr. G. L. Piper, and the resort's manager, Charles Brooker. This letter was filled with quite a bit of hype, but that wasn't unusual for the time.

It began with a description of the site, the origin of its name, and a repeat of the analysis of the water by the K. U. professors. This meant, said the letter's authors, that the springs could help with stomach aches. The waters also had "decidedly purgative" qualities in large quantities (bathing? drinking?), and therefore could cure "dyspepsia, indigestion, liver complaint, chronic constipation, kidney troubles, impurities of the blood, scrofula, constitutional disease, skin trouble," and so on. Dr. Piper had moved his sanitarium to the site and his practice was "supplied with all the new and approved appliances for the comfort and treatment of patron and patients."

Yet this was not all offered at the new resort. Mr. Brooker had "greatly improved" the Hotel El Dorado with new furnishings and decor to aid both the sick and simple traveler. The management also "spent considerable money" to beautify the park. There were better campsites, tent rentals, hammocks, and there was good fishing in the nearby streams. "You will live longer and happier for having spent your vacation at this lovely place and partaken of the health giving waters," the letter assured its readers. It closed with endorsements from travelers, doctors, and researchers, all of whom said that Chingawassa Springs compared favorably with springs and parks around the country.

The trains kept running to the resort that year as always. The June 24 issue of the *Record* lists four daily scheduled runs for the railroad. The first train left for the resort at 7:15 AM, then started its return to Marion at ten. The next three Marion departures were at 11:30 AM, 2:00 PM, and 5:30 PM. The trains leaving Chingawassa headed out at one, four, and eight PM. Interestingly, an October timetable in the *Times* was off by about half an hour on all but the 2:00 PM run. Another interesting point in the *Times* letter of June 23 was that patrons staying in Marion would get a free fare once a day when traveling from town to the resort. Those staying at the resort would get a reduced rate, and there appears to have been special rates for "picnic parties" at the park.

There was another Fourth of July celebration at the resort in 1892. According to the *Times* it carried just under 2,000 people there. It did so without breaking "arms, legs, necks or machinery." This was due to engineer Frank Wright, "who holds the lives to the throttle valve of the dummy engine." This suggests that there was some sort of arrangement between the locomotive and the dummy so that control of the former could be maintained from the cab of the latter. Considering that bi-directional control of diesel locomotives was still decades in the future, this was either a brilliant bit of mechanics or a desperate make-do improvisation that miraculously never failed.

Such an arrangement may have been the reason for the announcement that appeared in the July 14 issue of the *Times*. Manager Brooker seemed certain that the promise of the springs could be fulfilled if enough money was put into both the resort and the railroad. Therefore the newspaper stated that he was proposing a capitalization project costing over $100,000.

The project would involve the railroad, the resort, the allied Elgin Hotel in Marion, and the town's electric plant. The plant would allow for the electrification of the railroad. This would eliminate the need for the locomotives, as trains would be operated as electric trolleys.

The money would allow for the construction of a larger hotel on site along with rental cottages for longer stays. By including the power plant the resort and the railroad would have all the electricity they needed.

The newspaper reported that Brooker already had support from some Wichitans who were willing to take $50,000 in bonds to support the work. He was also getting encouragement from the "many distinguished visitors" to the resort that the effort would make Chingawassa Springs a paying venture. The newspaper's editor, C. E. Foote, thought that Brooker's plan was "feasible" and urged his readers to rally community support for it. Probably to that end in that issue and in later issues Foote published the comings and goings of visitors to the resort.

One of the former employees of the railroad was able to recall a few interesting items about its operations. In addition to carrying stone from the quarries, he said that the railroad would also bring boxcars to farmers along the route to make it easier for them to load the grain. Another time in the autumn an engineer forgot to top off his locomotive with water before making a run back to Marion. He had to stop along the way at the author's place to get water from the well, leading to the sight of a locomotive being filled with pails of water. Finally, the man wrote that he was able to hold off a run long enough for he and his future wife to change their clothes to attend some sort of formal event.

But then, very suddenly, outside events ended the fun of the little railroad and the big dreams of its owners. A financial panic struck the nation early in 1893 resulting in the failures of banks, railroads, and many other businesses. Investors lost fortunes and ordinary people lost their jobs. In such an economic environment it would have been impossible to keep the Chingawassa projects going.

What's unusual about this isn't so much that it happened, but that so little was reported in the Marion newspapers about Chingawassa's demise. All the *Times* said was, on July 27, that 25 workers were tearing up the track in preparation for its removal. On August 4 the *Record* stated that the railroad was "no more" but the resort remained open. In fact the resort may have remained open for some time, as there was a brief story about it in a 1902 issue of the *Record*. The quarries the railroad served also remained in business for several years, but eventually they went the way of the railroad and the resort as well.

According to later researchers the hotel building was eventually dismantled and converted into a barn. The ties went to a local farmer who used them as fence posts. No one seems to know what happened to the locomotive and the dummy, but the two passenger cars became community fixtures. One of them became the foundation of the "Owl Car" restaurant, which earned that name because it was open all night. The Owl Car seated eight until 1961. A new owner expanded the restaurant and the car went to an area farmer. The other passenger car served as a doctor's office until it too was moved to a farm.

Incredibly, this second car has survived to the present. This author was informed of its discovery during the research for **Ghost Railroads of Kansas**. It was moved from its rural location into Marion for preservation. Unfortunately the man who was spearheading this effort died. The car sits in town, patiently waiting to learn its fate. Aside from a few stock certificates and tickets in storage at the Marion Historical Museum, that car is the only survivor of the Marion Belt & Chingawassa Springs railroad. There are no photographs or paper records still in existence.

It's possible that this little railroad might not have disappeared so completely. Had the Panic of 1893 not happened, or had not occurred when it did, Brooker's big improvement project might have gone through. That could have kept the resort and railroad going well into the Twentieth Century. Who knows? Chingawassa Springs might well have become as famous a resort as its backers hoped it would be.

Still, for the few years it operated, the Chingawassa Springs railroad was unique. Its main purpose was to carry travelers to a resort. This gives a distinction among Kansas' more colorful railroads. It was a pioneer a century ahead of its time.

Postscript: This article was read by members of the National Orphan Train Museum, which was in the process of moving to Concordia, Kansas. They acquired the MB&CS coach in 2005 and moved it next to the Union Pacific depot, where there museum is. Plans call for the coach to be given a prototypical appearance to help tell the story of the "orphan train" riders.

THE SAINT JOSEPH & TOPEKA:
KANSAS' FIRST GHOST RAILROAD

The St. Joseph & Topeka railroad holds a singular distinction in Kansas history. It was the first railroad in this state to be abandoned in its entirety. This makes it Kansas' first "ghost railroad," in that both the company and its line disappeared.

Unfortunately, finding information on this line's brief history has not been an easy task. Issues of newspapers that might contain important facts have not all survived to the present. No one left an account of working for this railroad. References to it in local histories are sparse. Yet, with what remains, along with what is known about railroading of the time, it's possible to construct a coherent story of this short-lived but remarkable little railroad.

The story begins as the territorial era of Kansas history was coming to an end. Several communities in and around the territory were backing railroad projects to advance their own prosperity. The St. Joseph & Topeka was incorporated by the Territorial Legislature on February 20, 1857. It seems to have been backed by both Kansas interests and businessmen in St. Joseph, Missouri.

St. Joseph, along with Kansas City, Leavenworth, and Lawrence, aspired to be the metropolis of the Central Plains. It had already thrown support to a project known as the Marysville, Palmetto & Roseport Railroad. The MP&R was to build between St. Joseph and Marysville. In 1860 it would lay the first track in Kansas, a four-mile segment from Elwood to Wathena in Doniphan County. In 1862 the line would change its name to the St. Joseph & Denver City, and later the St. Joseph & Grand Island. It was under this third name that the line would come under the influence and eventual ownership of the Union Pacific.

The St. Joseph & Topeka and the MP&R appear to have been tied together early on. The MP&R was to connect St. Joseph to the booming Big Blue River valley of northeastern and north-central Kansas. The St. Joseph & Topeka was planned to link both those cities, giving St. Joseph access to the western parts of the Kansas River valley. What's interesting about this is that both cities had been on opposite sides of the slavery controversy. St. Joseph was one of

Missouri's staunchest pro-slavery towns; Topeka had been founded by abolitionists and had become the political center of the antislavery movement.

By the start of 1859 the issue of slavery in Kansas was settled. In January of that year a Topeka newspaper threw its full support behind the project. It proclaimed pleasure that the people of St. Joseph had already subscribed to $50,000 of railroad stock, was confident that Doniphan County would subscribe to more, and believed that in Topeka almost $100,000 would be raised to build the line. The newspaper even called for St. Joseph businesses to advertise with it in anticipation of the swift completion of the railroad. The main question at the time was whether a direct route should be attempted, or if the line should go through Atchison and then to Topeka.

It's here that the story becomes murky. Nothing was done about the project during the Civil War. From other histories it's clear that Topeka became more interested in the Atchison & Topeka (later the Atchison, Topeka & Santa Fe). It's also clear that St. Joseph put its efforts into maintaining the first railroad into the city, the Hannibal & St. Joseph, and in promoting the St. Joseph & Denver City. The St. Joseph & Topeka railroad didn't disappear during this time; it became dormant as the attention of its two terminal cities went elsewhere. But it appears that in Doniphan County the railroad remained an important idea.

This was probably due to the need of two of the communities in the county, Doniphan and Wathena, for a railroad. Doniphan had been founded in 1854 by proslavery men from St. Joseph. It was located along the Missouri River, and quickly prospered due to the riverboat trade. Its politics also broadened; in 1858 it was briefly home to the *Crusader of Freedom*, a newspaper started by James Redpath and allied with Jim Lane. However, trade from the river slackened after the Civil War, and the town would need a railroad if it was to survive.

Wathena by contrast seemed to have no political sentiments one way or the other. It was founded in 1856 on a site four miles west of the Missouri River and ten miles east of Troy, the seat of Doniphan County. It was an ordinary frontier town that began to grow after the Civil War. It was already going to be along the SJ&DC, so folks here may have wanted the St. Joseph & Topeka as a second railroad to make their community more prosperous than Troy.

It's a few years after the war that the story of the St. Joseph & Topeka picks up again. According to an 1882 plat book of Doniphan

County, "the company was organized in 1869." As the St. Joseph & Topeka already existed, this may have been in fact a reorganization of the railroad. But it's also here that the story again clouds up.

That same plat book states that in 1870 the Doniphan County commission gave the St. Joseph & Topeka $200,000 of SJ&DC stock. This was apparently a funding measure; the railroad would sell the donated stock to raise cash for construction. The commission stipulated that the donation was made on the condition that the company "would have the road completed from Wathena to Doniphan inside of one year." But a 1905 history of the county reported that construction didn't begin until 1872. Whenever construction got underway, the total length of the line from Wathena to Doniphan was thirteen and one-half miles.

Newspapers of the time are not helpful in straightening out this conflict. Although newspapers were being published in Troy and Wathena at this time, the issues have not survived to the present. Issues of the *Atchison Daily Champion* from the summer of 1870 hint at the earlier date for the construction of the St. Joseph & Topeka. On May 20, in a report on the prospects of Doniphan County for settlement, the *Champion* reported that the county "has in running order and in point of completion as many Railroads as any in the state." The following month a brief notice on all the railroads in operation in Kansas didn't mention the St. Joseph & Topeka, but did state that with the number of railroads being built, mileage in Kansas was expected to go up from over 1,200 then to between 1,700 and 2,000 miles before the year ended. On the other hand, there's a *Champion* story from August of 1873 that refers to the St. Joseph & Topeka, stating that it had been "completed over a year ago." This suggests that it might have been built late in 1871 or in early 1872.

Whichever source is right, once the St. Joseph & Topeka was up and running it did fulfill it's original mission. The line was part of a direct route from St. Joseph to Topeka. Ominously, though, it was only a small part of that route. From St. Joseph to Wathena riders took the SJ&DC, then the St. Joseph & Topeka to Doniphan, the Atchison & Nebraska from Doniphan to Atchison, and the AT&SF from Atchison to Topeka.

It might be helpful here to mention the progress of these other railroads up to 1873. The A&N was finished a few years earlier. Its route went from Atchison through Doniphan and White Cloud to Lincoln, Nebraska. This line was part of James Joy's Chicago,

Burlington & Quincy railroad system. The AT&SF had reached the western border of Kansas in 1872, which was the same year the "original" line from Atchison to Topeka was completed. As for the SJ&DC , it had reached Marysville in 1871 and was coming under the influence of railroad financier Jay Gould.

The railroads of Doniphan County,
including the St. Joseph & Topeka

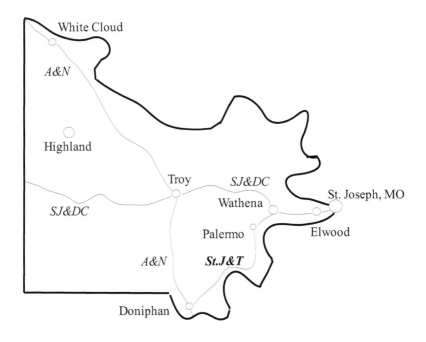

It's also in 1873 that the name "Kansas City, St. Joseph & Council Bluffs" appears in connection with the St. Joseph & Topeka. The 1905 Doniphan County history states that the St. Joseph & Topeka was leased to the KCSJ&CB. The Atchison Champion of August 10, 1873 makes reference to the KCSJ&CB in connection with the Burlington & Missouri. The B&M was a Missouri railroad that was part of the Joy system. These suggest that the St. Joseph & Topeka was also part of the Joy system.

Whatever the case, it's here that the Wathena newspaper enters to shed light on operations of the St. Joseph & Topeka. Two stories in early October make reference to the railroad. The first notes that a spot on the line south of the village of Palermo was a frequent hazard for local livestock. More cattle and hogs were killed there, where the railroad and a local road paralleled, "than on all the balance of the track between Wathena and Doniphan." The newspaper urged that the railroad fence its right of way there both for local stock owners and for the traveling public.

The second story was related to the first. It reported that someone had recently dumped a pile of logs onto the track not far from Palermo. Because of the location the newspaper speculated that the dumping was related to a loss of livestock. "This is one of the few acts for which people deserve hanging," stated the *Wathena Reporter*. While it conceded that the railroad's management seemed frustrating in relation to the local problem, such dumping only put railroad employees and passengers in danger.

Another hint of trouble on the railroad came in the spring of 1874. It seems that state tax assessors misnamed the company the "Wathena & Doniphan" while making note of the taxes the company owed for 1873. The railroad's managers tried to use this error to avoid paying any taxes. The *Reporter* suggested that this effort was related to the fact that the railroad's operational lease was due to expire later that year. The State Legislature therefore passed an act to legalize the assessment. The *Reporter* also noted that because of the "filibustering" of management, a ten percent penalty was added to the assessment.

The following year the situation for the St. Joseph & Topeka became worse. It seems that there was a problem with the track between Wathena and Palermo. In March of 1875 the county commission told railroad management to either fix the problem or face legal action. The railroad was seized by the sheriff in April and put up for sale early in May. As no buyers came forward, the company was placed in the hands of a receiver, A. H. Horton of Atchison, who was to run the railroad until ordered otherwise by the county court. James Joy's B&M railroad took over the lease and operated the line through the summer and early fall. In October the B&M gave notice that it intended to discontinue operation of the St. Joseph & Topeka on November 1, 1875.

These problems may have been related to another that was mentioned in the 1905 Doniphan County book. That text stated that the St. Joseph & Topeka bonds were "placed with a firm of New York brokers," probably around the time of construction. "Before the bonds were disposed of," the book continued, "the firm failed and the bonds were taken by its creditors as assets and foreclosed." This may have also figured in the seizure by the county sheriff.

But this may have not been the end of the railroad. An issue of the Wathena *Reporter* for March 18, 1876 contained a story on why Wathena was an ideal town for emigrants to Kansas. Newspapers of this time were filled with such stories. But in this one in particular, one of the advantages noted was that Wathena was at the junction of the SJ&DC and the St. Joseph & Topeka. While this might mean that the railroad was still in operation, it could also be just boosterism on the part of the newspaper. After all, it was better to claim that the town was at the junction of two railroads rather than to state that it only had one.

But the end was near for the little railroad; it appears to have been abandoned in 1878. The reason why, aside from it's clearly poor condition by then, isn't entirely clear. The most likely reason for its failure is that it was a bridge line. It wasn't long enough to have much on-line traffic, so for its revenue it had to rely on freight and passengers going from St. Joseph to Atchison or Topeka. But it didn't have its own line to those two Kansas cities. This made it vulnerable to collapse if viable alternate routes were constructed. They were built while the St. Joseph & Topeka was being constructed or shortly thereafter. This made the road's demise an inevitability.

According to the 1905 book the railroad was taken over by the SJ&DC. This is backed up by a souvenir book in the Kansas State Historical Society that covers the SJ&DC predecessor company, the St. Joseph & Grand Island. This book states that the the SJ&DC acquired the rails and used it on its lines to the west of the area. The book adds that railroad financier Jay Gould purchased the right of way.

This makes sense, as Gould became interested in the SJ&DC during his battle with Union Pacific management in the late 1870s. Gould later sold the right of way to the Chicago, Rock Island & Pacific.

The Rock Island never used the right of way for any of its lines in Kansas, though the purchase suggests it might have considered the possibility. Maps in the 1882 plat book hint that parts of the right of way became local roads. The whole right of way might have remained intact into the Twentieth Century. There may have even been an effort around World War One to revive the line as an electric interurban railroad.

In time, though, the St. Joseph & Topeka faded away. When the *Topeka Capital-Journal* published a short piece on the railroad in 1968, it did make the connection between the territorial project and the first tracks laid in Kansas along what became the SJ&DC. But it incorrectly stated that the project died early in the Civil War and was never built. The St. Joseph & Topeka also cropped up in Congressional testimony in 2000. When Michael J. Ogborn, Managing Director for OmniTRAX, testified in July of that year before a House Subcommittee about an "Emergency Small Railroad Preservation Act," he noted that the St. Joseph & Topeka was the "first [railroad] abandonment in Kansas."

This fact is sad in one way: the area it traversed is now both scenic and historic. If it had survived to the present, the railroad might have made a good excursion line. Riders on its trains could have learned about many aspects of state history, from "Bleeding Kansas" to the riverboat trade to the late 1860s settlement boom. But the St. Joseph & Topeka didn't survive, so it isn't famous. It's infamous as the first Kansas railroad to be given up as a failure.

TWO RAILROADS, TWO TOWNS, AND ONE RUDE SURPRISE

Abandonments of railroad lines are today a fact of modern business. Railroad companies cannot operate on lines that aren't profitable to them. If they can't find a company willing to offer service along that route it's abandoned.

But railroads can't give up lines on their own, without giving anyone notice. The federal government has to be notified along with customers on the line in question. An effort to find an new operator must be undertaken. The tracks can only be taken up with the approval of federal regulators.

This was not the case back in the Nineteenth Century. Then companies could do as they pleased with their lines and no one, not even the national government, could interfere with their decisions. Such decisions could prove unpleasant shocks to communities along these lines who needed railroads in order to survive. In the spring of 1881 such a shock hit Anthony in Harper County, and it could have proved fatal to that city.

The story of that shock begins early in 1879. On February 11 the Leavenworth, Lawrence & Galveston Railroad filed a charter with the state to form the Southern Kansas & Western railroad. The charter specified that the company's line would start in either Independence or Thayer, along the LL&G, and build west. Plans called for the line to run through Elk County and Cowley County to Winfield, then to Wellington, then to Harper in Harper County, and ending at Medicine Lodge in Barber County.

Both the *Sumner County Press* in Wellington and the *Harper County Times* in Harper printed news of the filing in their issues of February 20. The newspapers reported that the board of directors of the new company included a mix of Boston capitalists and men from Elk, Cowley, and Sumner Counties. A few weeks later the *Anthony Journal* reported on this news, and along with other planned railroad construction to the county, urged its readers to "'brace up,' make all necessary improvements," and "prepare for the reception of the 'iron horse.'"

What's interesting about the SK&W plan is that at the time Harper and Anthony were engaged in a fight over the seat of Harper County. Harper managed to win an election in the fall of 1879 and capture the seat. However, the supporters of Anthony raised cries of fraudulent voting, and the location of the seat was still in question. Both towns had their hopes of becoming the ultimate victor.

Although the SK&W favored Harper for an east-west rail line, Anthony was not left out. The Atchison, Topeka & Santa Fe railroad had constructed a branch line to Wichita in 1872. Under the name "Cowley, Sumner & Fort Smith" it extended that line south to Arkansas City, and also built a line from Mulvane to Wellington, all in 1880. That same year the "Sumner County Railroad" built from Wellington to Hunnewell. In all likelihood it was also around that time that it created the "Wellington & Western," which was to build from Wellington to Anthony.

By the summer of 1880, and perhaps as early as 1879, the SK&W had reached Wellington. Shortly after the Fourth of July, construction began on the SK&W at Wellington for the push to Harper. The Harper County *Times* of July 15 was jubilant at its prospects. It gleefully reported that not only was the SK&W not going to Anthony, but that the W&W might not come there either. "Now is the time for men to invest and start in business here," the newspaper proclaimed. "We do not know of a town in Southern Kansas that can offer the inducements offered by Harper at the present time."

Yet on that same day the *Anthony Republican* reported that the extension of the Santa Fe there was "an assured fact." The next day the other Anthony newspaper, the *Journal*, stated that construction of the W&W was to start on July 19. The head of the Santa Fe's construction efforts was quoted as having "always said" that the W&W "would be the first into Harper [C]ounty and he rarely fails to fulfil [sic] his promises."

On July 22 both the *Press* in Wellington and the *Republican* reported that track-laying on the SK&W had already gotten underway. A week later the *Times* stated that grading of the SK&W had gotten to within six miles of Harper. That same day the *Press* stated that a telegraph line was going up parallel to the line.

There was plenty of news about both lines on August 5 and August 6. The *Republican* reported that track on the SK&W was being laid at the rate of one mile a day; that the W&W was graded to the Harper County line; and that the Santa Fe planned to extend its line to Medicine Lodge. The *Press* also stated the latter, along with news that track-laying on the W&W had begun on August 4. The *Journal* noted that W&W surveyors were at work in Harper County.

The railroads of Sumner and
Harper Counties, 1880

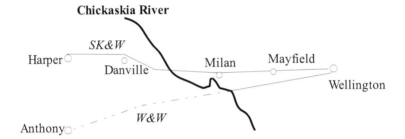

One week later there was more news in the *Times*, the *Press*, and the *Republican*. In the *Times* was an SK&W public timetable. Train No. 1, a passenger train, arrived in Wellington daily at 10:40 PM, while No. 2 left daily at 5:00 AM. No. 11, a freight, was to arrive five minutes ahead of No. 1, while No. 12 was supposed to leave Wellington daily at seven. In the *Press* was news that the town of Mayfield in Sumner County had just been created along the SK&W, while the Santa Fe was offering $1.50 a day to tracklayers for the W&W.

By far the largest story on the situation as of August 12 was in the *Republican*. It stated that the W&W had its abutments and piles for its culverts in place to the Chikaskia River. As to the bridge over that river, the company had framed timbers ready and a pile-driver in place to begin work. West from the river to the county line grading crews were building up the roadbed. In Harper County surveyors almost had their work completed so that the right-of-way could be condemned and handed over to the railroad.

For the rest of August all the news about both railroads came from the *Press*. On August 19 there were two important stories. The first was that a few days before the SK&W had hosted an excursion to Milan. The second was of an accident involving William Jackson, a construction conductor on the SK&W. Six days earlier Jackson had tried to jump aboard a locomotive while making a "running switch" at the Wellington depot. Jackson missed the foothold on the locomotive, fell, and had his right foot crushed so severely that it had to be amputated. A week later the Press reported some good news: the W&W track was now "fifteen miles west of the junction," or just southeast of the present-day town of Argonia.

On September 2 the *Times* reported that the SK&W could be expected in Harper in one week. The railroad had already graded for a long siding. It also planned to install a turntable, probably a temporary measure to turn locomotives, rather than a permanent structure that would have meant the location of locomotive servicing facilities in Harper. Still, the newspaper predicted that the town would boom as soon as the tracks arrived. Meanwhile on that same day the *Republican* stated that the W&W now had its route to Anthony, and the Press reported that the W&W tracks were "almost to the Chikaskia."

The next day the *Journal* told its readers that "satisfactory intelligence" had come to that newspaper to the effect that construction on the W&W was proceeding apace. Not only had the surveyors located the line to Anthony, it said, but they were also working "to find the most desirable location for a depot." "Anthony is to-day, and, with the Santa Fe road, will forever be the metropolis and county seat of Harper [C]ounty, as well as one of the most substantial and beautiful cities of the Southwest. No town in the State can beat it." Indeed, the road was reported to have reached the river the next day.

On Friday, September 10, the tracklayers of the SK&W reached the town of Harper. When the Harper County *Times* came out six days later, it was positively giddy about this news.

> "All shipments for the west, north and southwest must come to this point," it said, "and our merchants will furnish all this vast region with goods. The immense wholesale and most of the local trade that has been done at Wellington for the past year will now be transferred to Harper... All the cattle being held in the counties west and in the Indian Territory, (excepting raw Texas cattle) will be brought here for shipment... The indications now are that Harper will be the terminus of the road for the next year at least."

Such talk seems extreme, but the newspaper can be forgiven for some of its excessive rhetoric. The fact was that Harper, not Anthony, had a railroad line. Harper had so far held onto the county seat. In the middle of that September of 1880, it would have seemed to any observer that Harper's prospects were set and Anthony's were in considerable doubt.

This would have been further verified by an item in the Sumner County *Press* of September 16. "Work on the W. & W. railroad has been suspended," it read. "Diverse and sundry rumors have been afloat as to the cause and results of it; but nothing reliable is yet known."

The next day the *Journal* in Anthony seemed to have more certain information. It reported that an announcement had been made of a "compromise" between the leaders of the two railroads. The agreement was that the Santa Fe would "temporarily" surrender "this territory" to the SK&W.

> "The details of the arrangement are not yet known so that we cannot speak advisedly," it continued, "but we admit the

presumption that the A. T. & S. F. will not complete its track to Anthony, and will take up the track already laid, some fifteen miles in this direction. It is, of course, a serious disappointment to those who were counting on a real estate boom, but the business men take a very sensible view of it, that they would probably suffer less than they would if the road had come with its multiplication of business houses without a corresponding increase of patronage."

Furthermore, the newspaper wrote, trade in both Wichita and Wellington had not been strong, and Anthony still had other railroads planning to arrive in the near future. Locals were "never cast down or discouraged by back-sets" but would as always get up and work harder.

There were efforts later in the month by Anthony citizens to meet with officials of the SK&W. Such meetings were held and there was some speculation that perhaps that road would indeed turn south from Harper. But there was no firm word until the Republican reported in late November of rumors that the Santa Fe was about to acquire the LL&G.

The rumors were proved true in early December. A letter printed in the *Republican* had gone to stockholders in the LL&G and its family of lines. Sent from Boston and dated November 20, the letter told of an agreement between the Kansas City, Lawrence & Southern (the new name of the LL&G) and the Southern Kansas & Western, both of which would be folded into the Kansas City, Topeka & Western Railroad Company. The latter company was a proxy for the Santa Fe, which according to the agreement was to control the new KCT&W through stock shares. The move was, according to Santa Fe railroad historian Keith Bryant, an effort on the part of Santa Fe president William B. Strong to prevent a rival railroad from obtaining major lines in Santa Fe's home territory.

That was where matters stood until late April of 1881. On April 28 the Sumner County *Press* reported than an official of the Santa Fe had been in Wellington a few days before. "In an interview he stated that he had been directed to visit this point and investigate the condition of the company's affairs here," it continued, "with a view to the extension of the Wellington & Western road from the Chikaskia River, to which point it is now completed."

Two days later the *Republican* picked up on this news. It not only quoted the whole Press item, but added others to its own story. There had been rumors of the completion circulating for some time, it noted, but with this visit, along with a visit by another official and correspondence from Wellington, seemed to confirm the good news. "It looks as though our fondest hopes [are] soon to be realized," it said.

A week later the stories seemed to be coming true. "GLORIOUS!" proclaimed the *Republican*. Posters had gone up in Wellington reading, "Wanted, 200 men, $1.50 per day, and 300 teams, $3.00 per day, to work on the Wellington & Western Railroad. Apply to W. B. Strang & Son, Wellington, Kansas." Supposedly crews were already strengthening the river bridge in anticipation of new traffic over the line.

That this news was confirmation that the Santa Fe intended to complete the W&W was not simply accepted in Anthony. The May 7 issue of the *Republican* recounted stories in the *Wichita Eagle*, the *Commonwealth* of Topeka, the *Caldwell Post*, and the *Press* in Wellington, all of which said the same thing: the Santa Fe was at last going to finish the W&W and lay tracks into Anthony. The *Republican* noted the excitement was rushing through Anthony, and that businessmen, residents, and farmers were all counting on the coming of the railroad.

Then, on May 12, came the first stunning news in the *Press*: "The Wellington & Western Disappears in a Night."

It happened like this. At around one in the morning, Sunday, May 8, two construction trains left Wellington to head to the end of the W&W line. Two hours later the workers on those trains began to tear up the tracks and ties. The removal of material continued through Sunday and Monday until it ended sometime Tuesday. The track and ties were stored in Wellington, presumably to be used by the Santa Fe on some other construction project.

That the workers themselves didn't know what was going was reported in the other newspaper in Wellington at the time, the *Wellingtonian*. It stated this fact under a column of news from Milan that began with this: "What's up is the greeting. The Wellington & Western R. R. is the reply."

In Harper County the reaction was predictable. The Harper County *Times* of May 12 was jubilant. "That [the W&W] is the last hope of Anthony for a road everyone concedes," it stated. Harper had been discouraged by the prospects of the completion, but with line gone, Harper had undergone "such a sudden bound ahead that even her most ardent admirers are astonished." On the other hand, Anthony's "last effort" had been attempted "and has failed." Only Harper had solid business prospects and "for years" would be "the headquarters of trade for southwestern Kansas."

The *Republican* of May 14 was angry but unbowed. "That the Santa Fe railroad company have disappointed our people, is a fact," its story on the removal of the tracks began.

A few sentences on it stated, "Our people were deceived. Any other people would have been deceived under similar circumstances. As regards this operation of the company, it is unnecessary to comment. Its right to tear up the road is unquestioned. The deceptive manner in which it was done, is quite another thing. It may be in strict accordance with their ideas of right, but that is of no consequence to us now. They slapped us in the face in a vigorous manner; but at the same time transformed us from a state of doubt into one of absolute knowledge as regards what we may expect from their hands. In plain English, we can no longer look to the Santa Fe for connections with the outside world, and this being positively settled the way is clear for a united effort in another direction.

"The people of Anthony know no such word as fail. They have been deceived and disappointed, but the old vigor and pluck is still here--the determination to succeed in planting the banners of Anthony high in the heavens of southern Kansas. Hardly had the above operation been generally known before our citizens were devising ways and means for relief and already an interest has been awakened and plans matured for the future."

In the end Anthony would get other railroads. It would also get and hang onto the seat of Harper County. But for a time in the spring of 1881, folks there realized just how powerless they were in the face of a railroad corporation. No doubt it was a lesson that took them a long time to forget. Time marches on, of course, and these days railroads are not so powerful as they once were. But the lesson Anthony learned is one that we should take heed of. Who can say that it can't happen today in some other industry? Who's to say that we can't suffer due to the selfishness of others?

A RAILROAD AS A PAWN:
THE DODGE CITY, MONTEZUMA & TRINIDAD

Occasionally railroad projects of the Nineteenth Century were about more than just transportation. They could be efforts to boost one town over another. They could be part of one company's attempt to outflank a rival. At worst, they could be schemes to defraud honest folks out of their hard-earned cash. The Dodge City, Montezuma & Trinidad Railroad was one of these railroads founded for purposes beyond running trains. It was part of one man's plan to be a powerful person and one community's effort to gain political power, as well as being another community's lifeline to the world. The story of this line is one that deserves to be told and retold.

The story begins with New York businessman Asa T. Soule. Soule had become a wealthy man in the patent medicine trade. In the late 1880s he decided, for whatever reason, to create a financial empire on the booming American frontier. He chose western Kansas as the base of this empire. In short order Soule founded the Eureka Irrigation Canal and took control of the First National Bank of Dodge City.

For decades one of the ways to make money on the frontier was through the founding of towns. Selling town lots in a thriving city could make someone very rich. Soule was attracted to this method, and chose Gray County as the site of his new town. He named the town Ingalls for the powerful Senator from Kansas, John J. Ingalls.

But creating a town wouldn't be enough, if the effort was to profit Soule. Plenty of towns were being founded in western Kansas at the time. The best way to guarantee permanence to a town was to make it the county seat. Soule decided that Ingalls should be the seat of Gray County. However, the county already had a seat, the town of Cimarron. But that didn't keep Soule from spending money to buy votes and hire cowboys to assure victory in the contest to Ingalls.

To assure Ingalls' chances, that town would have to have allies in the rest of Gray County. There were two communities in southern Gray County, Ensign and Montezuma, that needed a railroad to build through them if they were going to survive. So to aid them, and to get them to aid Ingalls, in late 1887 Soule created the Dodge City, Montezuma & Trinidad railroad company. The plan was for the line to build from Dodge City, and its new connection to the Rock Island, through Ensign and Montezuma, and eventually on to Trinidad, Colorado.

Railroad meetings were quickly held in Montezuma to rally support for the project. The newspaper in town, the *Chief*, published letters from Soule and a Rock Island official stating that the project was on a firm footing. Grading on the railroad started in March of 1888, but progress was slow. The grade wasn't completed until June. The building of bridges also went slowly, and it wasn't until August that the track was finally laid to Montezuma. On Tuesday, August 21, 1888, the last rails were spiked down at Montezuma. The event was marked by a performance by the local band and a small celebration.

A bigger celebration was held a week later when the road was formally opened. On hand at that event were two photographers named Kurtch and Wood; speakers from Hutchinson, Dodge City, and Garden City; and the editor of the newspaper in Santa Fe in Haskell County. Because it had been raining off and on for the two days before the opening, the *Chief* eagerly stated that this "confirmed the theory that railroads bring rain and prosperity." An excursion train ran on the DCM&T from Dodge City to Montezuma.

Asa Soule was naturally the president of the new railroad. A man from Soule's hometown of Rochester, New York, Frank W. Dickinson, was vice-president. The secretary and treasurer was W. W. Munsell. The superintendent of the line was R. R. Hudson. The agent at Dodge City was John W. Gilbert; he also served as the company's auditor. The agent at Montezuma was A. H. Hudson, possibly a relative of the superintendent.

While service on the new railroad began immediately, it wasn't until November that the first timetable appeared in the Montezuma newspaper. The daily westbound train arrived at Montezuma from Dodge City at 1:05 PM. The eastbound train left Montezuma at 2:40 PM.

It was also around that time that Asa Soule finally came to Montezuma. He met with local citizens on his visit to assure them that the town was going to get a roundhouse. He promised that once construction resumed westward the town would be a division point on the line. These were efforts to buy votes, and no one was shy about that. At the end of its brief story on the visit, the *Chief* exhorted its readers to "vote the Ingalls ticket" to "show your appreciation" for Soule's efforts.

In Montezuma the railroad eventually had a depot, a water tower, a windmill, and an engine house. But though Haskell County voted for DCM&T bonds to extend the line, Montezuma remained the end of the railroad. The railroad was 26 and a half miles long. There's no surviving information on the DCM&T's equipment, though it seems that the Rock Island provided any locomotives and passenger cars.

There were several changes in the DCM&T's timetable made during the spring of 1889. The *Gray County Republican* of March 7 showed that the westbound left Dodge City at 11:40 AM and arrived in Montezuma around 2 PM. The eastbound left Montezuma at 2:40 PM and arrived in Dodge at 4 PM. By the end of the month this was altered so that the westbound train left Dodge at 7 PM, and the eastbound departed Montezuma at 7:30 AM.

Complaints were immediately registered in the newspapers in Santa Fe and Montezuma. The new schedule forced passengers to have to stay in Montezuma no matter which direction they were going. While this might have benefitted the hotel in Montezuma, people thought the change an inconvenience. Their complaints must have worked, for by the end of April the DCM&T's westbound train was now arriving in Montezuma around 12:30 PM, and the eastbound leaving there around 3:30 PM.

On Friday, January 17, 1890, Asa Soule died after becoming ill a few weeks before. His death was mourned by both newspapers in Dodge City and apparently throughout much of western Kansas. This was a blow to the DCM&T, but not a serious one. However, over the next few years the climate of western Kansas turned harsh. A drought struck the region, cutting into the farm traffic that was vital to the survival of the railroad. In addition a financial panic struck the nation in 1893, which led to businesses failing and farms being foreclosed.

The DCM&T was still in operation through the first part of that year. A timetable published in the *Dodge City Globe-Republican* at the end of March showed the railroad still running on the schedule it had chosen in April of 1889. Then in May a story appeared in that paper that revealed that the owners of the DCM&T had been in talks with Rock Island officials. The goal of these talks was to get the Rock Island to take over all operations of the DCM&T. There was no agreement at the time of the story, but it was reported that there were still shippers in Montezuma interested in maintaining service.

Days later a Garden City newspaper claimed that rumors circulating of the possible abandonment of the DCM&T were a ploy.

Officials of the line wanted Montezuma to vote more bonds to continue the line to Haskell County. Talk of abandoning the railroad was supposed to encourage support for the bonds. The *Globe-Republican* called this story "an erroneous supposition," and that no end of service was in the works.

However, the DCM&T timetable stopped appearing in that newspaper late in July. On August 4 notice was published that the road was to be sold in a receiver's sale at the Ford County courthouse at 10:00 AM on September 5. What was up for sale was the track, ties, roadbed, right-of-way, switches, and the depots the line owned. According to a later author, everything was sold to a cashier at the First National Bank of Dodge City, who was acting at the behest of a relative of Asa Soule's, E. E. Soule. Supposedly Soule knew of someone willing to buy the physical plant of the railroad.

The effort to tear up the DCM&T seems to have begun late in December of 1893. This caused considerable outrage in both Gray and Ford Counties. This wasn't so much because of the railroad disappearing, but due to the line owing back taxes to both counties. The *New West* in Cimarron reported on December 21 that only the week before had the DCM&T taxes for 1892 been paid. The newspaper expressed concern that if the abandonment went ahead the 1893 taxes would never be paid.

Days earlier the Ford County Commission held a special meeting on a Saturday to discuss the matter. They agreed to allow the county attorney to file an injunction against the abandonment. The injunction was to keep the assets of the DCM&T from being removed until the company's taxes for 1893 were paid.

In Gray County citizens filed a petition with the court asking for an injunction to prevent the tearing up of the line. The judge hearing the matter decided that an injunction was not "the proper remedy" for the situation. He did state that a mandamus could be filed requiring the road be operated, or that the owners could be sued for failure to pay back taxes. Following the ruling another judge issued a restraining order against the company preventing continued abandonment until another hearing was convened.

Newspapers in both Cimarron and Dodge City wondered if the owners of railroads could simply tear them up when they became "tired" of running them. There seemed to be no recourse for citizens and communities along these lines who had invested in bonds to initiate construction. Nor did there seem to be any recourse for counties when these railroads gave up the ghost and skipped out on their tax burden.

The case between Gray County and the owners of the DCM&T went before the State Supreme Court in January of 1894. Thumbing their noses at such legal niceties, while the issue of the restraining order was being heard, the owners' crews tore up the whole line in Gray County. An effort to intercept and impound the removed material failed. The county then tried to compel a rebuilding of the railroad, but this too failed. However, it wasn't until February of 1895 that the last of the railroad in Ford County was torn up.

What was once a promising project in the ambitions of one businessman had come to naught. So too did his effort to give power to the town he had founded, for Ingalls eventually lost its fight with Cimarron for the seat of Gray County. Montezuma did survive the loss of the railroad, but it had to move a mile and a half north when the Santa Fe built through the southwestern corner of Kansas.

Had the DCM&T been a bit more of a serious railroad, pushing farther west and south, it might have survived to the present in some form. But strange things happen when times are good. Enthusiasm overcomes common sense. Such might be the epitaph of this short-lived railroad.

THE SALINA NORTHERN:
THE LAST KANSAS RAILROAD

The last new railroad line built in Kansas was an 80-mile stretch from Salina to Osborne. It was constructed in 1915 and 1916 as the Salina Northern railroad. There were two other railroads built around that time, the Scott City Northern and the Anthony & Northern (Wichita Northwestern). But unlike those two lines, this line has remained in operation to the present. That makes this railroad's history worth telling.

That history goes back to the summer of 1910. At that time a new railroad project was established, the "Salina, Tipton & Northern." In mid-August a meeting was held in Osborne to present the idea to the public. Calling the meeting to order was Hal W. Neiswanger, an Osborne resident long interested in a railroad from there to Salina. Neiswanger introduced H. J. Palmer of Aurora, Illinois, a representative of the Securities Selling Company of Montreal. Palmer's company would sell bonds for the new railroad so the line could be built.

At the meeting Neiswanger revealed that a company had been chartered to construct the railroad. Heading this company was Cawker City resident John Hazeltine. The vice-president was Louis Tucker of Los Angeles; D. Mont Gantz of Cawker City was secretary; James Higgins, president of the Cawker City Bank would be treasurer; and U. G. Palmer of Illinois (a relative of H. J.?) was the general manager. Several people stated at the meeting that the railroad was needed, and pledges were secured to buy stock in the new ST&N.

Fundraising for the new line continued into September. Then in October it was revealed in the *Osborne County News* that control of the company had been turned over to "new people." The *News* didn't mention who the new leadership actually was. They continued to lobby for individuals and local governments to buy stock. For the next several months that's where matters stood.

In April of 1911 the *News* reported that one J. D. Landis of Philadelphia, "a personal representative of Eastern financial interests," was about to visit Osborne. Landis was coming to look over the region to be crossed by the ST&N on behalf of a group of investors.

The news story also stated that the ST&N leadership had been having problems finding reliable capital to build the line. But little else happened for many more months.

Then in November of 1911 A. P. Chamberlain, an investor from Des Moines, came on board the ST&N. Chamberlain held meetings to encourage stock purchases. He pledged that once enough stock had been subscribed construction would get underway. He voiced optimism that the road would become profitable once it was built and operating. By the end of the year bond elections for counties and townships along the proposed line, which would be used to buy stock, had been set for the new year. It appeared that at last progress was being made.

A story appeared in a Topeka newspaper that was picked up by the paper in Downs in January of 1912. It announced that the Atchison, Topeka & Santa Fe was planning to extend its Abilene-Barnard branch line to Osborne. The Osborne *News* was skeptical of the announcement. The Santa Fe, it said, had built this "dinky branch line" 20 years ago and had never before considered extending it. The scheme was the idea of a few large landowners around Barnard, and no one else. The only reason the Downs newspaper printed it, *News* editor Edwin Hadley claimed, was to put down the ST&N.

Later that month the bond elections in Osborne and Mitchell Counties went overwhelming in favor of the line. Yet on February 15 Hadley railed that too many locals were "indifferent" to the project. In April bonds were voted for the railroad in Salina, and businessmen there were reported to be fully supportive of the ST&N.

Hadley praised the ST&N again in June. The occasion was that another projected line, the Winnipeg, Salina & Gulf, was being sued in federal court in Topeka by a construction company. One man had been behind it, Hadley wrote, had made wild promises about investment, and had created "expensive offices" in Salina. This was not line the leadership of the ST&N, who were working to get actual investment to built a real railroad. By April of 1914, Hadley predicted, the line would have cars running between Salina and Osborne.

In August, October, and December readers of the Osborne *News* were promised that the last stock was about to be pledged and a survey of the right-of-way started. In January of 1913 Hadley urged his readers to be patient. In March it was revealed that A. P. Chamberlain was no longer with the company due to illness, but Hal Neiswanger was still hard at work. In May he stated that there might be a change in the ST&N. It might not be built as a steam railroad, but as an electric or "interurban" railroad, thanks to a new investor from Kansas City.

That was the last written about the ST&N for a year and a half.

Then in the autumn of 1914 things started to move again. First was an announcement in the Osborne *News* of October 22. It stated that "a proposition" for constructing the ST&N would be submitted to the public in three weeks. "This will be the former proposition reinstated," it added, "only on terms more favorable to the people." The statement was signed by Hal Neiswanger.

Formal notice of the changes to the project came out in mid-November of 1914. The *Osborne County Farmer*, picking up on a Salina newspaper story, reported on November 19 that the new railroad would be called the "Salina Northern." Frank C. York of Salina would be president of the new company. Hal Neiswanger was still involved, and he and York were joined by E. A. Tennis.

Tennis was president of the Keystone Construction company. The Farmer stated that he had recently built the railroad line from Garden City to Scott City and the Scott City Northern. Tennis was certain that he could get this new effort to connect Salina and Osborne completed.

He was also certain he could do so without the risks undertaken by the ST&N backers. He promised to keep the bonded indebtedness of the new line below $17,500 per mile. The SN would obtain financing through bonds rather than stock sales. This, said the Lincoln Sentinel, would be "better for the people" than what had happened with the ST&N.

Meetings were held in Salina on November 23 to discuss the new railroad. There was a morning meeting held for the general public, then a private one in the evening for the members of the Salina Chamber of Commerce. Doing most of the talking at both meetings was E. A. Tennis.

Tennis stated that plans called for the line to be completed to Lincoln by December 15, 1915, and to Osborne one year later. The line would mainly be a freight hauler, giving farmers of the region the option to send traffic through Salina. Tennis added that there would be some passenger service, either with a motor car (a "doodlebug") or with an extra car on freight trains (a "mixed train").

As far as investment went, Tennis stated that the company proposed that subscriptions be paid in first mortgage bonds. This would be different from the previous project which had solicited stock sales. If the road wasn't built the new subscriptions would never come due, which Tennis believed would make them a safe investment. Communities along the line would also have to make bond issues, and businessmen in Salina needed to take $100,000 in subscriptions if the railroad was to be constructed.

Both Salina newspapers were enthusiastic about the new project. For the next several days they reported on developments such as the signing of a contract between the first subscribers and Tennis' company, and the petition drive to have a bond election in Salina. In Salina the petition needed 2,000 signatures, and for a time it seemed that the goal might not be reached. But it was, and by December 1 elections for bond issued were set in every town and township along the proposed route.

On December 15 the Salina Northern Railway elected its first officers. F. C. York of Salina was chosen president; H. W. Neiswanger of Osborne was chosen vice-president; F. L. Brown of Lincoln County became secretary; Thomas Corpstein of Tipton became treasurer; and Thomas Brann, Junior, of Lincoln was elected chairman of the board. Also on that day officers were chosen for the Keystone Construction Company, the official contractor of the line. E. A. Tennis was elected president; two Salina men, a man from Salt Lake City, and a man from Denver were elected as officers. Both Keystone and the SN chose to be represented by the law firm of Ritchie and Spencer.

The election for local bonds was held as scheduled on January 4, 1915. The *Salina Journal* reported on that day that turnout was light. But although the balloting wasn't large, the bonds passed everywhere by safe margins. In Salina they passed 550 to 155. Similar results came in Smoky Hill and Glendale townships in Saline County, but in Ohio township the vote was 63-61 in favor. The Journal called this a victory because in the past such bond elections had gone against railroad projects.

In Lincoln County the vote was very overwhelming in favor of the bonds. The closest vote was in Marion township, and there they passed two-to-one. The two townships in Mitchell County voting passed the bonds unanimously. Finally, in Osborne County the bonds went through on a vote of roughly 430 to 50.

Officials of the railroad promptly promised to start construction as soon as possible. However, Salina investors still had to pony up $100,000 in bond subscriptions to make it a certainty. By the start of February about half that amount had been sold. The SN was allowed to start issuing stock at the end of March, and on April 5, 1915, construction of the railroad got underway.

Grading of the roadbed started a week and a half later. The *Salina Union* noted on April 17 that this work was enough of a novelty to attract viewers from Salina who would drive out to the grading site to watch the crews. The project also got the attention of the *Topeka State Journal*, which noted that not only was the route in place but so were sites for depots.

Work accelerated in May. In June it was announced that the SN would operate out of the new Union Station being built in Salina. At the same the road reported that tracklaying was set to start around July 1. On August 2 the SN earned its first dollar of revenue by switching cars from one railroad to another in Salina. Construction of the line led to the creation of two new towns, Hedville in Saline County and Westfall in Lincoln County.

In mid-August the SN announced that it would not use the new Salina station but build one of its own. The depot would be on north College Street, on the west side near the Missouri Pacific tracks. The reason for this was that the railroad needed offices as well as a station, and its building would serve both purposes. All seemed to be going well for the SN. In fact, on September 16 the *Union* reported on a meeting between Tennis, officials of the Midland Valley, and George Theis, Junior, head of the Arkansas Valley Interurban. The meeting dangled the prospect of the SN being extended south to Wichita.

But suddenly the project ran into a major obstacle: the Union Pacific. The SN had applied to the State Public Utilities Commission to be allowed to cross the UP tracks on the north side of Salina. At ten in the morning on September 17 commissioners visited the crossing site, and an hour and a half later they voted to grant the SN permission to cross. By noon SN workmen had removed the UP's rails and had laid ties.

The UP at that point filed a temporary restraining order, an injunction against further work, and, to make certain nothing more happened, they wrecked a locomotive at the site. UP officials claimed that they had not been given 30 days' notice of the meeting. They also claimed that the SN was not intending to hold up an agreement to keep gates that would block the SN and protect the UP line would always be kept locked. The UP's actions managed to delay its westbound freight and passenger trains.

The situation for the SN looked dire. The *Union* predicted that if the restraining order was made permanent the railroad "may be abandoned." The road would get tied up in so much litigation that it would be "almost impossible to continue construction." "It is absolutely necessary that the Salina Northern cross the Union Pacific tracks to get out of Salina," the newspaper concluded.

That evening officials of both roads met to try to hammer out their differences. SN officials agreed to erect the crossing gates if the UP would permit the crossing to be built. If the crossing was finished by the time a formal hearing on the restraining order was held the following week, the matter would be dropped at UP's expense. If it wasn't done, both sides would ask for a continuance to allow it to be finished.

To some degree, the Salina *Journal* noted on September 18, the SN was the winner and the UP the loser. The UP was chagrined to discover that it couldn't removed the derailed locomotive without a wrecker. What's worse, the newspaper reported, the UP didn't have a wrecker within 50 miles of Salina! In fact, the only wrecker that close belonged to the Missouri Pacific and was being used by the SN. When faced with the prospect of having their main line closed for ten hours, the *Journal* noted, or giving in to the commission, "Union Pacific officials decided the latter plan the better thing to do."

By the end of the month the crossing was complete. The SN then applied for another crossing of the UP at Lincoln. That too was granted, and construction carried on. However, one man lost his left hand and lower arm on October 11. Charles Kaser was helping to erect a bridge near Tescott when a pile driver came down on his hand. While he was a workman on the line, it appears his main job was running one of the cook shacks to feed other employees. His hand and arm were so badly crushed that they had to be amputated.

In the middle of the battle with the UP, a fascinating story appeared in the Osborne *Farmer*. On September 16 it reported that E. A. Tennis was in talks with the leadership of the Arkansas Valley Interurban. The AVI was an interurban connecting Wichita, Newton, and Hutchinson. At the time its leadership was considering expansion, and one of the expansion plans was a line to Salina.

Tennis was apparently in talks to join the SN with this AVI expansion. This wouldn't convert the SN into an electric line, though. The *Farmer* reported that if the combination occurred, parts of the new system would be electric, while others would be operated with motor cars. Of course, no grand alliance of Kansas short lines came about at the time. That would have to wait for another day.

On January 3, 1916, the tracks of the SN arrived in Lincoln. Bad weather had slowed the work, but now the first half of the system was completed. The next day the *Union* reported that freight operations between the cities were underway. Passenger service wasn't expected to start until February 1.

With that section complete the Salina city council issued $10,000 worth of SN bonds, the first half of its promise to the railroad. Late in January the SN moved into its depot and and offices in Salina. Otherwise work halted for the rest of the winter. It wasn't until early March that more rails and materials arrived to allow for resumption of the push to Osborne.

In mid-April a story in the *Journal* noted that the road was being "swamped" by demand for freight cars to handle a strong wheat harvest. Passenger service didn't start until a month later. It did so when two passenger cars from the Pennsylvania arrived on the line. One of the cars was described in the Journal as a "combination mail, baggage and smoker," the other as having a "spacious observation compartment in the rear with six large chairs."

Although two trains were run on the first day of passenger service, May 14, regular service called for only one daily train. It would leave Salina at 8:30 in the morning and arrive in Lincoln at 10:45. It would then depart Lincoln at 2:30 PM and return to Salina at 4:15 PM. This suggests that the railroad expected to carry more people to Lincoln than to Salina.

A few days earlier the *Farmer* reported on several developments on the SN. In Lincoln the railroad yard, switch sidings, a brick depot, and other facilities were being finished. "Eighty percent" of the grading between Lincoln and Osborne was done, and work on bridges was fifteen miles past Lincoln. Finally, it stated that revenue from freight traffic was enough to "pay all fixed charges and interest on its bonds" on the Salina-Lincoln section.

Another tragedy, much more spectacular than the October injuring, took place on May 21. The SN had a work camp at Hedville where several blacks employed in the construction were staying. One man was in the bunk house, lying on the floor, when another came in. The second man offered the sell the first, known as "Hoboe Jack," a pint of whiskey for a dollar. Jack and the other man started drinking, then the second abruptly demanded his money. Jack replied that he'd have to wait until his payday, a few days away. The other man refused to wait and pulled out a butcher knife. Jack drew his Colt revolver and shot the other man; he later died from his wounds.

This wasn't enough to slow construction. In June officials of the SN were hoping to make it to Osborne by September 1. But it seems weather and other problems slowed the effort. The tracks didn't reach Tipton until the middle of October. Problems again slowed the work, and in mid-November it seemed that Osborne wouldn't be reached for another month. But then the weather turned good, and the crews were able to lay track into Osborne at the end of the month.

In fact, it was on Thanksgiving Day, November 30, when the tracklaying was completed into Osborne. Many people turned out to watch, but there was no celebratory locomotive entrance. According to the *Farmer*, "miscreants disabled the donkey engine," disappointing the crowd. The construction crew got a break for a large Thanksgiving lunch.

The Salina Northern and Neighboring Lines, 1917

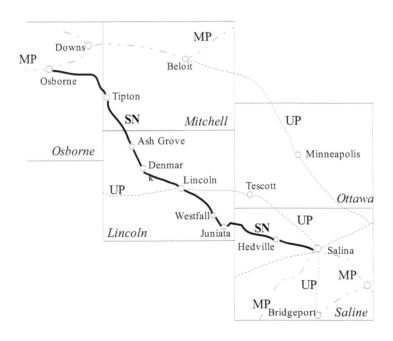

The first train into Osborne arrived the following Monday. It was a mixed train with freight cars and one of the SN's coaches. Former Osborne resident Chet Richolson bought both the first Salina-Osborne ticket and the first Osborne-Salina ticket. The tickets were returned to him so he could frame them. On December 4 the first timetable for Salina-Osborne service appeared in the Journal. Trains would leave Salina Mondays, Wednesdays, and Fridays at nine in the morning. Trains would arrive in Salina on Tuesdays, Thursdays, and Saturdays at 4:21 in the afternoon. Since the SN had been running daily trains just two months earlier, this service was probably due to the winter weather.

Winter also figured into the plans of Osborne residents to celebrate the arrival of the SN. On December 21 the *News* reported that the Business Men's Association had decided to postpone the railroad celebration until the spring. No one was going to "get any pleasure" from being "in the open air" during such an event in the winter, so the event was postponed.

Optimism abounded for the SN in the spring of 1917. In March and April both Osborne newspapers reported that SN officials entered talks with people in Kirwin in Phillips County. The plan called for the line to be extended northwest to Kirwin, both to serve another area without rail service, and to connect the SN with the Chicago, Rock Island & Pacific. The Rock Island connection would allow customers even more choices for shipping.

Also during this time Hal Neiswanger announced plans to acquire motor cars to use as locomotives. He called this "inter-urban service," although it's probably more proper to say he was planning an early version of mixed-train diesel service. Whatever it's name, the plan was that farmers could travel with their produce to market and return home with groceries in a single day.

But then disaster struck. In early June a severe storm dumped rain south of Osborne. Eleven bridges were washed out, and in other places the track was undermined. However, upon inspection it turned out that the bridges themselves were not damaged, but the track on the approaches to the bridges were. For the rest of June SN crews worked to repair the line and get it back into service.

That same month a story appeared in a Downs newspaper alleging that the SN was about to be taken over by the Missouri Pacific. The shops facilities in Osborne would be consolidated in Downs, and the line through Downs that ended at Lenora would be extended to

Denver. The story was mocked in the *Farmer* on June 21 as so much hot air from Downs.

Changes were brewing on the SN, however. The timetable in the July 4 issue of the *Union* had the daily train leaving Salina at 3:30 in the morning and returning at 4:15 in the afternoon. Around the second week of July a committee led by Salina resident and SN attorney David Ritchie called for a meeting of the SN bondholders.

It was at this time that the news came out that E. A. Tennis was about to enter bankruptcy. The effect on this and the SN was that Tennis would have to sever his connections to the company. He would also no longer be able to pay the $700,000 owed for completion of the line above the $1.5 million in bonds that had been issued.

On July 21 H. W. Goebel, president of the Commerce National Bank of Kansas City, Kansas (and head of the American Bankers Association), purchased the Salina Northern for $693,000. The purchase price was the same as the debt, and therefore the sale took the line out of the red. About a week later David Ritchie was quoted in the Farmer as stating that repair work was continuing and that passenger service to Osborne would be restored as soon as possible.

Goebel's group continued to operate the SN until June of 1924. On June 4 the line was sold to the Santa Fe. The Santa Fe pledged to make improvements to the physical plant and to maintain service. The Santa Fe continued to run trains on the line until 1993, when the line became part of several sold to Denver-based Omnitrax and operated under its "Central Kansas" shortline. In 2001 Omnitrax sold its Kansas shortlines to the Kansas company Watco, and the SN had a new operator, the "Kansas & Oklahoma."

This is where matters stand at the present. Watco may invest in maintaining the line, but it seems no decision on the line's future has been reached. Will the story of what began as the Salina Northern continue to the line's centennial? We shall have to wait and see.

THE KANSAS SOUTHWESTERN:
TWO RAILROADS, ONE BRANCH LINE

Usually if a railroad branch line changes owners, it's because a larger company has bought up a smaller one. Occasionally a line goes from one major railroad to another, like the parsing out of the Rock Island's lines in Kansas after that railroad went bankrupt. Then there's the case of the line that ran between Arkansas City and Anthony. It began as a branch of the St. Louis & San Francisco (Frisco), and ended as a branch of the Atchison, Topeka & Santa Fe. It's a remarkable story of success and failure along the southern border of Kansas.

The history of this line begins with the expansion of the Frisco into Kansas in the 1880s. The Frisco reached Wichita in 1880. A few years later it decided to build southwest from the Butler County village of Beaumont towards the Cowley County towns of Winfield and Arkansas City. In November of 1885 the Frisco made it to Arkansas City to great fanfare.

But Arkansas City wasn't to be the end of the line. A week before the inaugural excursion on the line the *Caldwell Journal* predicted that once Arkansas City was reached work would be "begun on the branch to Geuda Springs and Caldwell." The new branch, known as the "Kansas City & Southwestern Kansas Railroad," was going to turn west from Arkansas City.

The *Journal* began reporting on progress westward in the spring of 1886. In May the initial survey of the route was undertaken. By the end of the month the grading crew was nearing South Haven. Near that town they made an startling discovery. "The railroad graders," reported the *South Haven New Era* on May 29, "east of town, unearthed the skeleton of one of the aboriginal occupants of this country, at a depth of seven feet, a few days ago."

In June one obstacle appeared in the path of the KC&SWK, in the form of an anti-railroad petition circulating in one of the townships along the route. The *Journal* was highly critical of the effort. It suggested that not everyone was behind it, just an unhappy few, and that those few were "standing in their own light." But more interesting than this was that the criticism contained a hint that the Frisco was not just building a branch line. Twice the commentary suggested that the ultimate goal of the line was the Colorado coal fields.

Two months later, in August of 1886, the line was opened to South Haven. The *New Era* called the line the "Geuda Springs, Caldwell & Western." This is the only place where the name occurred. Usually most newspapers simply referred to the line as the "Border Road" or the "Border Line."

On September 2 the *Journal* hailed the completion of the line into Caldwell. This was the second railroad to enter the town; the Santa Fe had already reached there. Nor was this to be all; the *Journal* was confident that the Rock Island would be the third line into town (it would be). The newspaper was also certain that the Border Line would continue, and not just to Colorado, but would pass "over the plains of New Mexico" to create "a trunk line to the Pacific."

The new line was a "first-class road." The bridges were high-quality, the rails were "all steel and as heavy as any used" on any road in the state, and the grade was "light and the curves as low [as] could be made." The depot in Caldwell was the best on the line. Immediately there were separate eastbound and westbound freight and passenger trains in operation.

After Caldwell the next point set to be reached would be the new town of Bluff City in Harper County. Bluff City expected to be an important town on the new branch. A map of the community in one of the early issues of the newspaper the *Tribune* spelled this out. Bluff City would not just get a depot, but separate freight and passenger stations. There would be a small railroad yard, a roundhouse, and engine maintenance facilities.

The tracks arrived in Bluff City in January of 1887. A timetable published in the *Tribune* the following month showed that the daily eastbound passenger train left Bluff City at 6:30 in the morning. It left in Arkansas City at 8:20 and reached Beaumont around 11 AM. The westbound daily left Beaumont at 4:00 PM, and arrived in Bluff City four and a half hours later. The slow pace was probably due to the train also carrying mail in addition to passengers. In several of the towns along the line this was their only connection to the outside world.

Progress halted on the branch line for most of 1887. There was an accident on a construction train between Bluff City and Caldwell early in February, but since no one was injured it's unlikely to have been the reason for the pause. It wasn't until late December of that year that reports surfaced stating that work would resume. At that time it was still predicted to be extended to Colorado.

The line was apparently doing a brisk business. In February of 1888 the *Tribune* published a timetable with several changes. There were now two eastbound and two westbound daily passenger trains. No. 1 arrived in town at just after 9:00 AM and No. 3 around 8:45 PM. No. 4 left Bluff City at 6:30 AM and No. 2 at 6:20 PM. As far as the freight train went, the eastbound left Bluff City at 3:15 PM and the westbound arrived at just after 8:00 PM.

Frisco officials came to the region that same month to prepare for the extension of the line at least as far as Anthony. In March Anthony voted re-approved a bond issue to aid construction. (An earlier bond was never accepted due to problems between the Frisco and their construction contractor.) A survey of the route was completed in April, but it wasn't until the end of May that construction finally got under way. Grading of the ten miles between Bluff City and Anthony was finished early in June. Track-laying started on June 13, and within two weeks the work was done.

But in the meantime Bluff City was dealt a serious blow. Frisco officials decided in June that Anthony and not Bluff City would get the engine facilities for the line. The *Tribune* tried to rally the citizens to show support for the railroad. There was too much talk about getting revenge on Anthony, the newspaper said. "What we should do is act." There should be public meetings with Frisco representatives. Other railroads should be encouraged to reach town. But "sitting down, folding our hands and cursing Anthony" would only lead the city nowhere.

Bluff City appears to have weathered this loss well for the next few decades. The opening of the Cherokee Strip may have decreased the population somewhat, as did fires in several businesses in wood buildings in the early 1900s. Perhaps the biggest blow came when the Great Depression caused the local bank to move to Anthony. Today even the paved road through town is gone, and the population hovers around 75.

On July 5, 1888, the *Anthony Republican* published the timetable of the new line into the city. Westbound Passenger No. 1 arrived in Anthony at 9:45 AM and No. 3 at 8:45 PM. Eastbound No. 4 left at 6:50 AM and No. 2 at 5:30 PM. Also on the schedule were trains Nos. 29 and 30, "mixed" trains that carried freight but would also carry passengers with specific tickets or railroad passes.

For the next twelve years the branch line operated without

controversy. This changed by the autumn of 1896. A timetable in the *Arkansas City Traveler* for the Frisco tells readers of connections east and and west on its system. Significantly, though, the westbound connections aren't to Anthony, but to Burrton on the main line through Wichita. Indeed, the statement on routes for train No. 305 says that riders would take the train to Burrton to get to Anthony; no mention of the road's own line is made!

On November 3 the *Traveler* reported that the local Frisco agent said that the railroad wasn't planning on selling or leasing the branch line, but was going to buy it outright. This suggests that the Frisco was operating the line through the KC&SW rather than operating directly as part of the system. This would explain a brief opinion in the *Traveler* six days later stating, "The Frisco railroad west ought to be operated." The Frisco by this time wasn't helping the company operate the branch, but as the Frisco wasn't the direct owner or operator, the branch was languishing without service.

This is what was left of the Bluff City KS depot as of the early 1990s. The structure was clearly much wider, and may have been two stories tall. At the time the photo was taken, the depot was being used for storage by the local grain elevator. This is all that remains of the promise to Bluff City that it would be an important railroad town. *Author's photo.*

The next day, November 10, news came out that the Cowley County commission had been negotiating for a refund of the bonds issued to the KC&SW in 1885. The terms of the old bond issue called for a tax levy to maintain the funding of the bonds once ten years had passed. The commission felt it wiser to retire the old bonds and issue new ones at a lower interest rate than keep up the old bonds. Talks had gone on over the summer and in November new terms were agreed to. This seemed to close the matter, but in fact it was only a temporary peace.

On November 19 the *Traveler* reported that two Frisco officials had visited towns along the branch line to sound people out on the idea of abandonment of the line. "They were given to understand that the people are very sore over the treatment they have received," the newspaper said, adding that Anthony and other communities were preparing legal remedies to get the line into operation.

Late in November the action of the Cowley County commissioners over the KC&SW bonds became controversial as it appeared the branch might never return to operation. By November 29 Dwight Bramen, a New Yorker, had been appointed as receiver of the KC&SW. On that day he came to Arkansas City to inspect the line. He secured the use of a Santa Fe locomotive and passenger coach and traveled to Caldwell and back. To his anger he found that the Frisco had removed the line's handcars, tools, coal, and even the stationary in the depots. He promised people along the line that he would get it back into operation.

Over the next few days Bramen made arrangements for locomotives and cars for the line. By the second week of December Bramen had the line up and running again. Businessmen in Arkansas City hoped to extend it southeast into the booming Oklahoma Territory. There was track laid to Braman with the goal of reaching Blackwell, but the nine miles to Braman was all that was built. The line did take on a new name: it was now the "St. Louis, Kansas & Southwestern."

In October of 1898 a federal court ordered the sale of the line. It was now paying its expenses and therefore no longer needed to be in the hands of a receiver. It was sold at the Caldwell depot on October 21 to John Penman, a Canadian representing a group of bondholders from that country. Penman bought the line for $150,000. He was the only bidder on the line.

The line seemed to do well under the new owner. It's name was changed to the "Kansas Southwestern." A timetable in a January issue of the Anthony *Republican* states that there were two passenger trains running each way. Nos. 1 and 2 were through passenger trains and ran daily. Nos. 3 and 4 were accommodation trains than ran every day but Sunday (most likely as mixed trains). The through passenger trains were run in conjunction with the Frisco's passenger service, while the accommodation trains connected with the Frisco, the Santa Fe, and the Rock Island.

On July 12 the *Republican* reported that business was so brisk in Anthony that the KS had brought in a new locomotive and crew. There were two main reasons for the increase in traffic. First, the Kansas City, Mexico & Orient was building into town, and the KS was bringing them ties and other construction supplies. Second, the area was experiencing a large wheat harvest. The grain elevator in Anthony was taking in six to ten cars a day from the KS, the Santa Fe, and the other railroad in town, the Missouri Pacific. The KS itself didn't have very many freight cars, but it did have four locomotives and three passenger cars.

Late in August reports surfaced that the Santa Fe was purchasing the KS line. The reason for this, according to a report reprinted in the *Republican*, was to prevent the KS from extending its line to Fort Smith, Arkansas. The following month the superintendent of the line resigned and took a position with the Rock Island. The next month the Santa Fe assumed control of the line. According to Kansas Corporation Commission records the line wasn't formally merged into the Santa Fe until 1932. This means the Kansas Southwestern technically existed from 1899 to 1932.

Two years after the formal merger the first segment of the line was abandoned, from Arkansas City to Geuda Springs abandoned. In 1972 the track was removed from Geuda Springs to Metcalf. The last remnants of the line, from Metcalf to Anthony, were taken up in 1987. In almost exactly one hundred years the line had two major railroads as owners. It had promise under one, but became a backwater branch under another. Still, not every railroad can claim such a history, which is what makes the original Kansas Southwestern remarkable.

THE FIRST GROWTH PLAN:
THE RAILROAD CONVENTION OF 1860

These days we seem to have a myriad of "economic development" plans floating around to benefit our cities, counties, regions, or states. Some plans are fairly straight-forward and easy to support. Others pit vital interests against each other and lead to bitterness. This might seem like a modern phenomenon, but in fact Kansas' first attempt at a statewide economic development plan was made in the autumn of 1860. Like those present-day plans that cause controversy, that 1860 railroad convention was struck by division. Yet the routes agreed upon by all sides generally came to be built and operated.

One of Kansas's early governors, George W. Glick, noted that "railroad fever" struck Kansas Territory almost from the beginning. However, during the Territorial period "all railroad schemes were projected in the interest of some town or locality," Glick wrote, without any effort to consider a state system. These companies "were organized with millions of capital stock, but with no cash, no assets, and no office." For years little effort was made to unite the communities of Kansas around railroad projects. This was probably due to the battle over whether Kansas would enter the Union as a free state or a slave state.

To bring some order out of the chaos, and with the slavery issue largely decided, in the late summer of 1860 Edmund G. Ross, editor of the *Kansas State Record* in Topeka, began to lobby for a territorial railroad convention. The purpose of the convention would to hammer out an agreement on the railroad projects that would be of the most benefit when Kansas became a state. These projects would then be taken to Washington and federal aid would be applied to for all of them. Ross was joined in his call by John A. Martin, editor of the *Freedom's Champion* in Atchison.

A formal call was published in *State Record* on September 29 for a convention to be held in Topeka on Wednesday, October 17. Many of the major figures in Kansas politics at the time endorsed the measure. Free-state Republican Jim Lane and his free-state rival Charles Robinson joined in, as did former Territorial Governor Wilson Shannon and former proslavery partisan Benjamin Stringfellow.

Cyrus K. Holliday, one of Topeka's founders and a railroad backer, lent his name, as did one of the promoters of the Leavenworth, Pawnee & Western, James L. McDowell. Among the other recognizable names on this list were future Senators Samuel C. Pomeroy of Atchison and Preston Plumb of Emporia, and Santa Fe Trail legend Seth Hays of Council Grove.

According to the account publishing in the *Wyandotte Commercial Gazette* (Wyandotte is now part of Kansas City, Kansas), the convention was called to order at 10:00 AM on October 17 in Richey Hall in Topeka. Edmund G. Ross of Topeka was chosen temporary chairman. A committee then formed to prepare a list of permanent officers, with Benjamin Stringfellow of Atchison the chairman The appointment of this one-time violent opponent of the free-state movement was one of the signs that business affairs had taken prominence over the slavery struggle. The convention reconvened after lunch and W. Y. Roberts was elected president of the convention.

It was after this that the convention discussed the matter of representation, and promptly ran into trouble. According to the *Gazette*, the majority of those present wanted one delegate from each county. Those delegates in turn would vote on routes for a statewide plan. A minority wanted delegates selected on the basis of population.

In the view of the *Kansas State Record*, the majority felt that as the interior of Kansas needed railroads as much or more than the established towns, they ought to have as much say in the drafting of a state-wide plan. The discussion over the representation issue went on into the evening, at which point the majority plan was approved. That in turn led to the delegations from Leavenworth and Douglas Counties, along with their allies in other delegations, to walk out. They went to another place in Topeka to draft their own state railroad plan.

Ostensibly this withdrawal was due to the representation dispute. Contradicting this was a lengthy statement published in the *Commercial Gazette* in November by the convention's president, W. Y. Roberts. Roberts alleged that it was the backers of the LP&W who "bolted" from the convention because it was going to offer support to rival railroads, and the action hoped to sink the whole convention. He went so far as to call Thomas Ewing, Jr., one of the men running the railroad project, "the very leader of the bolters."

The very next day, as word of the walk out spread, the *Lawrence Republican* called the Topeka convention a "failure." The following week it blamed the breakdown of the convention on the aspirations of

Topeka men like Cyrus K. Holliday and Benjamin Stringfellow. "Stringfellow's convention," claimed the *Republican* on October 25, was intent on adopting a plan of railroads "in which the largest and most populous counties were completely ignored."

The strongest attacks on the delegate dispute came from the *Daily Times* of Leavenworth. It went further than the *Republican* on October 20, calling the regular convention "a fraud and a failure." The majority decision on the representation matter was, in their eyes, "unjust and unreasonable." That convention left Leavenworth "off the slate" while "showering bounties on Atchison and Wyandotte."

There might have been something to this. One of the projected lines that the delegates at the regular convention agreed to support was called the "Kaw Valley" route. This railroad would have started at Wyandotte (present-day Kansas City, Kansas); followed the Kansas River around but not through Lawrence and Topeka to Fort Riley; then roughly paralleled the Smoky Hill River west to the Rocky Mountains.

Its route was roughly similar to the one the backers of the LP&W were proposing. However, the LP&W was planned to start from Leavenworth. This isn't surprising, since most of the directors of the company were from that city. It may well be that Ewing and the other LP&W men did have something to with turning the delegate issue into a major controversy.

There were four other proposed lines that gained support at the Richey Hall convention. One was the "Atchison & Topeka," which was to connect those two cities, but at the convention was suggested to be extended to follow the Santa Fe Trail. The second, the "Jefferson City & Neosho Valley," was to start near Junction City or Fort Riley, extend through Council Grove and Emporia, then enter central Missouri to terminate at Jefferson City or St. Louis. Next was the "Lawrence & Fort Gibson," which was to run from Lawrence south through the Indian Territory and Fort Gibson to Galveston, Texas, on the coast of the Gulf of Mexico. Last came a line that was projected to start in Atchison and run through several northern counties and terminate at the western state line, but could be extended to the Pike's Peak region of Colorado.

Meanwhile, at the Chase House in Topeka, the alternative convention drafted their own plans. Strangely enough, the plan drafted by the bolters was remarkably similar to the one the convention passed. Virtually the only change was that the Chase House plans centered the state railroad system on Leavenworth. Indeed, the resolution drafted there said almost nothing about a railroad system and only addressed the attendees' grievances. It listed all the "unjust" actions taken and the population of the counties "harmed," but in the end its plan lacked the specifics of the plan drafted at the main convention.

With both conventions over, newspapers in Kansas began reporting on the results and trying to gain support for one side over the other. Naturally enough, the *Kansas State Record* of Topeka praised the work the regular convention completed. "The system adopted will at once recommend itself to the consideration of every reasonable man," it said. As to the bolters, the newspaper added, "We sincerely regret the course" they took. The *Record's* editors believed it had "resulted from a misapprehension of the temper and intention of the majority" that they might not have been fair to "every section of the Territory." "That the result arrived at will be satisfactory to nearly the entire Territory, we have not the least doubt."

The Routes Adopted by the
Railroad Convention of 1860

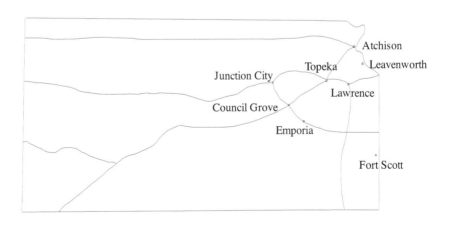

The *Commercial Gazette* in its issue of October 27 was largely favorable to the plan drafted by the convention. So was the *Western Kansas Express* of Manhattan, which on October 20 it called the convention "a great success" and hailed the system agreed upon. Also supportive was the *Freedom's Champion* of Atchison. In its October 27 issue it stated that the bolters "came there determined to agree to nothing, and they followed out that policy all through." "The plan of roads proposed is the best ever devised for Kansas. They run through every portion of it" and "penetrate into almost every county." "Our people should go to work, and by every means and influence in their power, endeavor to secure grants of land from Congress for these roads."

There was also negative reaction to events. Perhaps because its community was left out, the *Fort Scott Democrat* said nothing about the convention, good or bad. The *Neosho Valley Register* of Burlington, in noting the division, commented: "Thus the termination of this convention has verified our anticipations of what it would be, viz: a humbug." The *Emporia News* repeated the *Republican's* call that the convention was a "failure." But it didn't blame the LP&W faction; instead, it was Topeka's delegation that was to blame. They had 45 delegates present, while Leavenworth, three times their population, had only 10. Topeka and their allies in Atchison were behind the trouble because, claimed the *News*, they wanted the "lions [sic] share" of the land grant benefits of new railroad projects and "to deprive all other places" from obtaining those benefits.

The *State Record* responded to these criticisms in its October 27 issue. As to representation, it stated that the sparsely-populated interior counties had as much right to determine the results of the convention as the bigger cities. As to the plan adopted, the *Record* noted that twenty-nine of the Territory's counties would be "traversed" by at least one line, and that several would be at the junction of two or more lines As to any bias towards Topeka, the newspaper wrote that Shawnee County would receive a junction, but so would Douglas, Morris, Anderson, and Davis (now Geary) Counties.

The *Lawrence Republican* continued to be critical of the convention for the following few weeks. In its November 8 issue, it went so far as to accuse one of the newspapers that had backed the convention, the *Record*, of downplaying the number of Douglas County men in attendance. The *Record* had not only listed the Topeka delegates, but the names of attendees from Topeka as well. But why, asked the *Republican*, did it "not treat Douglas county the same way?"

The *Record* refused to let the charges of a bias for Topeka stand without comment. On November 3 it stated that a reading of the minutes would show that Topeka delegates had repeatedly mentioned Leavenworth as the starting point of some of the railroads. Had the Leavenworth delegates remained, their city would have fared better Furthermore, while the "entire trade of this section" had gone to Leavenworth, that city's railroad planners had not granted Topeka "a single act of partiality or favor," keeping the routes of their lines north of the Kansas River and bypassing Topeka.

The *Record* also engaged the newspapers that had attacked the convention. It singled out three, the Emporia *News*, the *Junction City Statesman*, and the *Republican*. The *Record* pointed out that the regular convention's plan favored both Emporia and and Junction City, while the bolters' plan bypassed the former and granted only one line to the latter. As for the *Republican*, the *Record* noted that under the convention plan Lawrence would be the starting point of the Galveston line, while the bolters had that point be Leavenworth.

Benjamin Stringfellow was later tasked to bring the memorial passed at the convention to Congress. But as it happened, every projected line was to be built by a separate company. That meant that the general unity of thought that conceived of a statewide railroad system quickly broke down. Each company sought to create its own system, and to make its own place in a system of regional and national railroads. Yet with one exception, the lines agreed upon at both conventions were in fact built.

That one exception was the Jefferson City & Neosho Valley. As George Glick noted years later, this company "had no friends after the convention adjourned." Indeed, this line seems to have come out of thin air. There doesn't appear to have been any reason for it, except perhaps that its backers wanted a route to St. Louis that bypassed Kansas City. However, the segment of the JC&NV from Junction City to Emporia ended up being the initial main line of the Missouri, Kansas & Texas.

Two other lines proposed at the conventions became much less important than their backers had hoped. The line west from Atchison was slow to start due to that city not having enough local capital for construction, and not being in as ideal a location as those towns around Kansas City. This line was built as far as north-central Kansas, but only managed to be a branch line of the Missouri Pacific.

The other line to suffer a similar fate was the Lawrence & Fort Gibson. A company was formed, the Leavenworth, Lawrence, & Fort Gibson, and it managed to lay the first track south of the Kansas River early in 1868. But the company was shortly thereafter paralyzed by division between local and out-of-state directors. It only got as far as Coffeyville, and became a branch in the Santa Fe system.

At the time of the conventions, the Kaw Valley route was thought to be the most important to Kansas, and for a time it was. The LP&W managed to secure the first grants of land along the right-of-way. Its named was changed to the Union Pacific, Eastern Division, and it laid track across much of the state after the Civil War. In 1869 the name was changed again to the Kansas Pacific, and it became the first railroad to cross the state and the first to enter Denver from the east. The KP profited from the Texas cattle trade that first terminated in Abilene.

But the KP was saddled with serious problems. Successive managements had buried the railroad in debt. Once the cattle trade moved to terminals along other lines its operations began to lose money. The KP and the Union Pacific engaged in a war over freight rates that made the KP's financial condition worse. Early in 1880 the UP took over the KP as part of a complex transaction carried out by railroad baron Jay Gould. Since the KP connected to major cities, Kansas City and Denver, its route is a main line in the UP system.

Then there was the Atchison & Topeka. During the Civil War Cyrus Holliday, its leader and main booster, added "Santa Fe" to the name. Holliday wanted the line to capture the lucrative trade of the Santa Fe Trail. To that end, after the war he was able to push the AT&SF to be the second railroad to build across Kansas. It also managed to steal the trade of the Texas cattle drives from the KP and profit from the move.

Successive leaders of the AT&SF didn't keep their visions confined to Kansas. They pushed the railroad west to Los Angeles and the Pacific Coast. They built east to Chicago, making the AT&SF the only national railroad with its own transcontinental line. They had branches built throughout the Midwest to open up traffic sources from grain to airplanes. They also assembled a popular schedule of passenger trains that lasted into the 1960s. The AT&SF remained a strong corporation until 1995 when it merged with Burlington Northern to form BNSF. It hadn't been planned that way, but the Atchison & Topeka ended up being the most important railroad in Kansas.

Of course, one look at the map of lines both conventions created shows one glaring feature. While several lines crossed the northeastern quarter of Kansas, the western two-thirds of the state only get two main lines, and south-central Kansas is bypassed entirely. How could this be?

At the time few thought white settlement would extend very far west of Junction City or southwest of Emporia. It just didn't seem worthwhile to project more railroads into regions of Kansas that weren't going to be settled.

Just as important a factor in these plans was the vision of trunk lines. It was believed that the only lines of importance were trunk lines connecting Kansas to the East, the Gulf of Mexico, or the Pacific. Few if any realized that branch lines that fed traffic into main lines would be vital to both opening the state to white settlement and to the financial security of railroad companies. It was the branch lines that gave the state the high number of railroad route miles that it would eventually have.

Still, it's interesting to look at how people in 1860 thought about a railroad system for Kansas. It's important to understand that the convention split in two, and to consider why that happened. To progress forward, we need to learn the lessons the past teaches us.

THE FRISCO'S SHORT-LIVED
HALSTEAD BRANCH

Mention the words "Frisco" and "northwest end" to someone who knows about Kansas railroads, and they'll probably recall that the Frisco (St. Louis & San Francisco) used to have a branch line that ran from Wichita to Ellsworth. What they wouldn't know, nor would anyone else who hadn't read every book on the Frisco, was that in the 1880s the northwest end of the Frisco was Halstead in Harvey County. Until now little was known about this branch, sometimes called the "Harvey County Railroad." Here is its fascinating story.

The story begins in the late 1870s. The city of Wichita had been served by the Atchison, Topeka & Santa Fe railroad for a number of years. City leaders felt that if Wichita was to grow, the ATSF needed some competition. They persuaded the managers of the Frisco to extend a line entering southeast Kansas to be extended northwest to Wichita. Construction began in earnest in 1878, and by the end of May of 1880 the Frisco had reached Wichita.

About four months later, on September 16, the *Wichita Eagle* reported that Frisco survey crews were working to locate a branch line from Sedgwick, north of the city on the Harvey-Sedgwick County line, to Halstead, several miles west of Newton. Both towns were already on the ATSF. Sedgwick was on the line from Newton to Wichita, while Halstead was on the main line running west out of Newton.

In order for the Frisco to run on this proposed line, it would need trackage rights from the ATSF. "Trackage rights" is a railroad term that means one railroad company is allowed to run trains on the line of another company. The *Eagle* story didn't say why the Frisco was interested in constructing this branch. Nor did it hint as to whether the Frisco intended either point on the branch to be the end, or if the line would continue past those points.

Nothing more was mentioned about the branch until March 17, 1881, when the *Eagle* reported that the Frisco had renewed their interest in the line. Two months later two stories in the *Halstead Independent* reported that the project was about to start. The first, on May 20, stated that construction would soon get underway. The second, dated May 27, reported that a contract to build the grade had been signed. But that was the end of the matter until the middle of autumn.

Then on October 14, the *Independent* announced, "Clear the Track!" A dozen engineers had arrived in the area earlier in the week. Two days before the newspaper came out, tools had arrived and the men had started laying out the stakes to mark where the grade and the track were to be. Although winter was around the corner, the newspaper predicted that Halstead would have its second railroad within forty days.

A week later the *Independent* carried an interesting little item. It noted that one "Miss Jennie Rhodes" of Granville, Ohio, was in town to visit her brother Dusty Rhodes and his family. Why is this interesting, and relevant? Because Mr. Rhodes was reported to be a "Locating Engineer" on the ATSF and was "engaged in setting grade stakes on the new line from Sedgwick to Halstead."

Over the previous year or so the Frisco and the ATSF had become corporate allies against their rival railroads. The Frisco had a land grant that would allow a company it owned, the Atlantic & Pacific, to construct a line across northern New Mexico and Arizona Territories. ATSF management wanted to build their own transcontinental line to the Pacific, namely to Los Angeles, California. The Frisco allowed the ATSF to take joint ownership in the A&P, hoping that the alliance would also give them the transcontinental line they desired. It was no doubt due to this alliance that allowed for the cooperation on the line to Halstead.

A few weeks later a story in the *Eagle* hinted at what else the Frisco might be up to with the branch it was working on. Earlier a bond issue for Sedgwick County had been proposed that would have given funds to the Frisco to build a line west from Wichita to the western part of the county. Opposition to the bonds, led by the rival newspaper the *Wichita Beacon*, had defeated the proposal.

"Now for the sequel," the *Eagle* stated on November 3. A Frisco official had been in the area recently. He announced that the Frisco might be willing to build a branch from Augusta, east of Wichita in Butler County, northwest along the Whitewater River to Newton. Such a line would give Newton as many railroads as Wichita, and could therefore diminish the city's chances of growth. The line was of course never built, but for a time the story probably made some Wichitans very nervous.

In the meantime work continued on the Halstead extension. On

November 11 the *Independent* reported that a Frisco official already had a silver spike on hand to drive when the tracks were laid. The main grade was finished by the first of December, and track-laying was mostly completed by the middle of the month. The line was officially completed and opened for initial operation on January 1, 1882.

This work brought some immediate benefits to Halstead. Both the ATSF and the Frisco erected a "Union Depot" for passengers and freight. The Frisco built its own water well, and a few other facilities. The town gained a second telegraph line, and towards the end of February gained direct mail service to Wichita. Not everyone was happy, though; a letter from Sedgwick published in the *Independent* on January 20 complained of high fares, long waits, and rude Frisco conductors.

The first timetable for the line appeared in the *Independent* on April 7, 1882. Passenger train No. 20, the "St. Louis Express," departed Halstead daily at 6:35 AM. No. 19, the "Texas Express," arrived daily at 8:05 PM. The daily eastbound freight left town at 7:25 AM and the daily westbound arrived at 12:20 PM.

Until now the only mention that had even been made of the branch was in the book **Frisco Folks** by William Bain, published in 1960. Bain's book isn't really a history of the Frisco. It's more a collection of anecdotes and stories the author picked up from older railroad employees. There are no sources in the book, so it can difficult to figure out if a particular tale came directly to the author, or was told to him from someone who had heard the original.

The story about the branch Bain related supposedly came from an "old timer." The man said that "the last three miles" of the branch as it went into Halstead "was considerably downhill." A train going to Halstead would then turn "a short curve" then run parallel with the ATSF to the junction. The switch leading to the junction was placed right past the bridge over the Little Arkansas River just east of town. "When you was [sic] at the switch stand you could look right down 30 feet or so into the river," the old timer said.

This was a scary proposition for trains operating in the days of hand brakes. A train that was going too fast, or one that hit the switch when it was in the wrong position, could easily derail into the river. This meant that freight crews had to be alert to problems, and that could make them jumpy.

One night, the old timer said, the freight got into Halstead late at night. With no where else to sleep, the men filed into the caboose to bed down. During the night a "Santa Fe fast freight" barreled through. The two lines being so close, the rumbling of the other train was both heard and felt in the Frisco caboose.

That woke up one of the brakemen, a man named "Nic." The brakeman, perhaps drowsy and still being nervous, awoke assuming that the rumbling was his train about to derail! He bolted awake and yelled, "Come on boys! She's goin' in the river!" He raced out of the caboose and onto the roof, and began setting the brakes on all the freight cars. It seems that it took him some time to realize the truth, and the old timer said that he was needled by his fellow Frisco men for quite a while afterward.

The Halstead branch seemed to do fairly well for at least five or six years after it was opened. Late in 1885 the *Eagle* observed that the Santa Fe was missing an opportunity by not using it as a way to filter traffic from central Kansas into Wichita. A timetable in another Halstead newspaper, the *Herald*, that was published in January of 1887 shows that by then three trains were running each way daily: a freight, a passenger, and a mail and express train. A notice in the *Beacon* in May of 1888 stated that the Frisco was adding a chair car, sleeping car, and dining car to its service on the line for central Kansas travelers going east of Wichita.

However, not long after that the branch's fortunes changed. Back in 1886 a group of local businessmen and Frisco officials had formed the Kansas Midland railroad. The KM's plan was to build a line from Wichita to Red Cloud, Nebraska. Fund-raising went for about two years, with construction getting underway in 1888. The KM's line went from Wichita through Burrton in Harvey County to Lyons, and ended at Ellsworth on the Union Pacific. Although initially an independent road, the KM was closely tied to the Frisco, and eventually would be taken over by the Frisco after 1900.

During the first year the KM was in operation, service on the Halstead branch was cut back to two trains a day. In September of 1889 the lease on the operation of the branch was about to run out. The Frisco chose not to renew the lease. The *Beacon* predicted that this would benefit the KM and, though the older line crossed "one of the richest parts of Kansas," it was a helpless branch and had to go.

Interestingly enough, this was the same sentiment expressed in the Halstead *Independent*. Yes, it conceded, some residents would move and others would lose their jobs. But the "Frisco road" had "never been an important factor" in the town's growth. "Nearly the entire business of our city has been done by the Santa Fe," and the loss of the branch was not going to have much of an impact.

However, the tracks on the branch weren't torn up right away. One week later, on September 20, the *Independent* reported that the Frisco's move had upset the ATSF. Officials of the latter road were now refusing to make a connection with the former at Burrton, were refusing to accept freight there, and were even tearing up "all of the platforms and other improvements" the Frisco had made when it had built through the town. For a month the two railroads remained at odds. Finally in mid-October an agreement was reached and a connection at Burrton made. It's probable that not long afterward, the tracks from Halstead to Sedgwick were removed.

So ends the story of the original northwestern extension of the Frisco, the railroad that billed itself as the "Southeast-Southwest" connection. What might have been the beginning of another, and perhaps quite important, line never amounted to more than an eight-mile strip of track. Such are the vagaries of old-time railroading.

BIBLIOGRAPHY

An Error in Timing:

Frisco Folks, Stories of the steam days on the Frisco Road, by
William E. Bain; Sage Books, Denver, 1961.
Augusta Weekly Gazette: July 22, August 12, December 9, 1898.
Walnut Valley Times: December 7, 1898; December 8, 1898.
Wichita Beacon: July 18, 19, December 8, 10, 1898.
Wichita Eagle: July 17, August 4, 9, 19, 24, 1898.

Trolley to the Oilfields:

The Electric Way: Arkansas Valley Interurban, by Robert
Collins; South Platte Press, 1999.
Augusta Daily Gazette: April 16, May 2, 3, 10, 22, June 9, July 25,
September 6, 28, December 21, 1917; February 14, 1918.
Douglass Tribune: April 27, May 4, 11, 18, 25, June 15, August 3,
10, 31, September 14, 28, October 20, November 2, 1917; July 16,
1920.
El Dorado Republican (Daily): April 16, May 10, 1917; February
14, 1918.
El Dorado Republican (Weekly): April 20, May 4, 11, June 15,
September 14, December 21, 1917.
Walnut Valley Times (Daily): April 16, 1917.
Walnut Valley Times (Weekly): September 14, 1917.
Wichita Beacon: February 29, 1916; April 16, July 21, September
5, 1917.
Wichita Eagle: April 15, December 21, 1917; July 8, 1920.

Otto P. Byers:

A Standard History of Kansas and Kansans, written & compiled by William E. Connelley, 1918.

Wheat Belt Route, by Lee Berglund; South Platte Press, 1998.

"Personal Recollections of the Terrible Blizzard of 1886," by O. P. Byers; **Kansas Historical Collections**, Volume 12; 1912.

"The Conception and Growth of a Kansas Railroad," by Otto Philip Byers; **Kansas Historical Collections**, Volume 12; 1912.

"Early History of the El Paso Line of the Chicago, Rock Island & Pacific Railway," by Oliver (Otto) Philip Byers; **Kansas Historical Collections**, Volume 15; 1919-22.

"When Railroading Outdid the Wild West Stories," by Otto P. Byers; **Kansas Historical Collections**, Volume 17, 1926-28.

Hutchinson Herald: April 8, 1936.

Hutchinson Record: April 10, 1936.

Kinsley Mercury: November 9, 1933.

Kinsley Graphic: April 9, 1936.

Larned Chronoscope: April 9, 1936.

Larned Daily Tiller and Toiler: April 8, 1936.

Pratt Daily Tribune: April 8, 1933.

"Samson of the Cimarron":

Faded Dreams: More Ghost Towns of Kansas, by Daniel C. Fitzgerald; University Press of Kansas, 1994.

Iron Road to Empire, by William Edward Hayes; publisher unknown, copyright 1953.

Southwest Daily Times: August 8, 1938; July 9, 1939; "Railroad used 'Samson' to put tracks out of Cimarron River's reach," by John Hanna, November 29, 2000.

Stories from unnamed newspaper, courtesy of Lidia Gray, Liberal: October 26, November 4, 6, 8, 15, December 15, 1938.

The Saga of the Scott City Northern:

Ghost Railroads of Kansas, by Robert Collins; South Platte Press, 1997.

History of Early Scott County, by the Scott County Historical Society, Inc.; copyright 1977.

Russell Springs Leader: April 1, May 6, 13, 1919; June 24, July 1, 8, 22, August 26, September 23, October 7, November 25, 1910; January 6, 20, February 10, March 10, 24, 31, May 12, 26, June 16, 23, July 7, 14, 1911; January 1, May 16, July 4, 25, August 8, 1913; February 23, March 9, August 31, September 14, 28, October 5, 12, 19, 26, 1917; November 9, 16, December 21, 28, 1917; January 11, February 1, 1918.

Scott City News Chronicle: June 17, July 1, August 5, November 18, December 16, 1910; February 3, July 28, 1911; February 21, May 23, June 6, 20, August 8, November 6, 1913; November 8, 22, December 18, 1916; January 3, October 3, 10, 17, 24, 31, November 7, 14, December 12, 1917; January 30, 1918.

Scott County Republican: February 16, June 22, July 6, 1911; January 16, April 24, 1913; November 23, December 14, 1916; January 18, February 1, 15, May 15, June 28, July 5, 26, August 2, September 20, 28, October 4, 18, November 15, 22, December 20, 1917.

Sabotaged by Fate and Greed:

Kansas West, by George L. Anderson; Golden West Books (Pacific Railroad Publications), 1963.

Kansas Pacific: An Illustrated History, by Robert Collins; South Platte Press, 1998.

"Early Days on the Union Pacific," by John D. Cruise; **Kansas Historical Collections**, Volume 11, 1910.

"Samuel Hallett and the Union Pacific Railway Company in Kansas," by Alan W. Farley; *Kansas Historical Quarterly*, Vol. 25, No. 1, Spring 1959.

"Thomas Ewing, Jr., and the Origins of the Kansas Pacific Railway Company," by David G. Taylor; *Kansas Historical Quarterly*, Vol. 42, No. 2, Summer 1976.

Kansas Daily Tribune (Lawrence): July 29, 30, 1864.

Wyandotte Commercial Gazette: July 30, 1864.

"Another Terrible Massacre":

Ups and Downs of an Army Officer, by Col. George A. Armes; publisher unknown; Washington, D.C., 1900.

Ellis County Gold, by Blaine E. Burkey; Thomas More Prep, Hays, 1979.

Kansas Pacific: An Illustrated History, by Robert Collins; South Platte Press, 1998.

The Buffalo Soldiers - A Narrative of the Negro Cavalry in the West, by William H. Leckie; University of Oklahoma Press, 1967.

Fort Hays: Keeping Peace on the Plains, by Leo E. Oliva; Kansas State Historical Society, 1996.

"A Point of Interest Along the Old Kansas Pacific," by H. A. Riebow; *The Union Pacific Magazine*, December 1922.

"When Railroading Outdid the Wild West Stories," by Otto P. Byers; *Kansas Historical Collections*, Volume 17, 1928.

"When the Union and Kansas Pacific Built Through Kansas: Part Two," by Joseph W. Snell and Robert W. Richmond; *Kansas Historical Quarterly*, Volume 32, Number 3; Autumn 1966.

Emporia News: August 9, 1867.

Junction City Weekly Union: August 10, 1867;

Kansas Daily Tribune (Lawrence): August 9, 10, 11, 1867.

Leavenworth Daily Commercial: August 10, 1867.

Leavenworth Daily Conservative: August 4, 6, 7, 11, 1867.

Leavenworth Daily Times: August 6, 1867.

Topeka Tribune: August 16, 1867.

Hays Republican: October 13, 1906.

"Railroaders' Graves at Victoria Recall Indian Massacres of 1860s," by Mollie Madden; *Hays Daily News*, December 16, 1956.

"Massacre marker returns to rightful home," by Beccy Tanner; *Wichita Eagle*, June 5, 2003.

The Marion Belt & Chingawassa Springs:

Ghost Railroads of Kansas, by Robert Collins; South Platte Press, 1997.

Marion County Kansas Past and Present, by Sondra Van Meter; published by the Marion County Historical Society, 1972.

"The Story of Chingawassa Springs," by Lucy Burkholder; no

date, archives of the Marion Public Library.

"Marion Co. Dreamed of Prosperity in Chingawassa Springs, Quarry Siding and Rainbow Lake," by Lucy Burkholder; *Marion Record-Review*, September 14, 1944.

"Memories Of Old Chingawassa Railroad And Resort," by Al Nienstedt; *Marion Review*, September 10, 1941.

Marion Record: February 1, 8, March 8, 22, 29, April 19, 26, June 7, July 12, 19, August 2, 30, October 20, 1889; March 21, April 4, June 6, 1890; July 4, 10, 1891; January 29, June 17, 24, July 1, August 26, November 18, 1892; August 4, 1893; August 1, 1902.

Marion Times: July 9, 1891; June 23, July 7, 14, August 4, October 20, 1892; July 27, 1893.

The St. Joseph & Topeka:

Railroad Abandonments in Kansas Before the Transportation Act of 1920; Kansas Corporation Commission, February , 2004.

St. Joseph & Grand Island Souvenir, bound book, archives of the Kansas State Historical Society.

Historical Plat Book of Doniphan County, Kansas; published by J. S. Bird, Chicago, Illinois, 1882.

Ghost Railroads of Kansas, by Robert Collins; South Platte Press, 1997.

History of the State of Kansas, by William G. Cutler; published by A. T. Andreas, Chicago, Illinois, 1883.

Doniphan County History: A Record of the Happenings of Half A Hundred Years, by Patrick Leopoldo Gray; The Roycroft Press, Bendena, Kansas, 1905.

Kansas Tribune (Topeka): May 15, 1858; January 1, 1859.

Atchison Daily Champion: May 20, June 23, August 10, 1873.

Doniphan County Republican (Troy): August 16, 1873.

Wathena Reporter: October 2, 1873; March 12, 1874; March 6, 29, April 10, May 8, 15, October 9, 1875; March 18, 1876.

Topeka Sunday Capital-Journal: February 18, 1968.

Testimony of Michael J. Ogborn, Managing Director, OmniTRAX, Inc.; On H.R. 4746, The Emergency Small Railroad Preservation Act; House Committee on Transportation and Infrastructure, Subcommittee on Ground Transportation, July 25, 2000.

Two Railroads, Two Towns, and One Rude Surprise:

History of the Atchison, Topeka, and Santa Fe, by Keith L. Bryant, Jr.; University of Nebraska Press, 1982.

Ghost Railroads of Kansas, by Robert Collins; South Platte Press, 1997.

History of the State of Kansas, by William G. Cutler; published by A. T. Andreas, Chicago, Illinois, 1883.

A History of Railroad Construction and Abandonment within the State of Kansas, December 1995 update, Kansas Corporation Commission.

Anthony Journal: March 6, 1879; July 16, August 6, September 3, 17, 1880.

Anthony Republican: July 15, 22, August 5, 12, September 2, 23, November 20, December 4, 1880; April 30, May 7, 14, 1881.

Harper County Times (Harper): February 20, 1879; July 15, 29, August 12, September 2, 16, 1880; May 12, 1881.

Sumner County Press (Wellington): February 20, 1879; July 22, 29, August 5, 12, 19, 26, September 2, 9, 16, 23, 1880; April 26, May 5, 12, 1881.

Wellingtonian: May 12, 1881.

Dodge City, Montezuma & Trindad:

Cimarron New West: December 21, 1893; January 4, 11, 25, March 8, 1894; February 21, 1895.

Dodge City Democrat: March 10, September 1, 1888; January 18, 1890.

Dodge City Globe-Republican: January 22, 1890; March 31, May 5, 12, July 28, August 4, December 22, 1893; January 5, 26, 1894; February 15, 1895.

Gray County Republican (Montezuma): March 7, 28, April 25, 1889.

Montezuma Chief: January 20, February 3, February 10, March 23, 30, May 11, June 8, July 27, August 24, August 31, November 2, 9, 1888; April 12, 1889.

"Soule's Road - A History of the Dodge City, Montezuma & Trinidad Railway," by Robert D. Dickerson; *Sparks*, the newsletter of the Topeka Chapter, National Railway Historical Society, June 2000.

The Salina Northern:

Ghost Railroads of Kansas, by Robert Collins; South Platte Press, 1997.
Lincoln Sentinel: November 19, 1914.
Osborne County Farmer: November 19, 1914; September 16, December 30, 1915; January 6, May 11, October 19, December 7, 1916; June 7, 21, July 12, 19, 26, 1917.
Osborne County News: August 18, 25, September 8, October 20, 1910; April 6, November 9, 16, 23, 30, December 28, 1911; January 11, 25, February 15, April 18, 25, June 6, August 8, 15, October 3, December 5, 1912; January 16, March 20, May 22, 1913; October 22, 1914; January 7, April 15, September 30, 1915; May 11, 25, October 5, December 7, 21, 1916; March 1, April 19, 26, July 12, 19, 1917.
Salina Daily Union: November 24, 25, 26, December 5, 15, 16, 1914; January 6, March 30, April 1, 5, 12, 17, May 11, 26, June 5, August 2, 12, 14, September 11, 16, 17, 18, 20, 23, 28, 1915; January 3, 4, March 2, May 15, May 22, October 3, November 16, 30, December 1, 7, 1916; July 4, 21, 1917.
Salina Evening Journal: November 23, December 15, 1914; January 4, 5, February 2, September 14, 18, October 1, 12, 1915; January 24, March 1, April 19, May 15, June 19, November 16, December 1, 1916; June 4, 1929; July 27, 1933.
Topeka Daily State Journal: April 13, 1915.
Wichita Eagle: "Possible rail deal cheers shippers," by Phyllis Jacobs Griekspoor, March 17, 2001; "Short lines plan merger," by Phyllis Jacobs Griekspoor, April 3, 2001.

The Kansas Southwestern:

Faded Dreams: More Ghost Towns of Kansas, by Daniel C. Fitzgerald; University Press of Kansas, 1994.
The St. Louis – San Francisco Transcontinental Railroad, The Thirty-Fifth Parallel Project, by H. Craig Miner; University Press of Kansas, 1972.
Anthony Daily Republican: December 28, 1887; March 20, April 9,

May 23, 31, June 6, 13, 22, 30, 1888; January 4, July 12, August 23, 30, September 27, November 1, 1901.

Arkansas City Traveler: November 25, December 16, 1885; November 3, 9, 10, 19, 27, 28, 30, December 1, 2, 5, 1896; October 22, 1898.

Bluff City Tribune: December 30, 1886; January 20, February 3, 10, 1887; February 2, June 30, 1888.

Caldwell Journal: November 19, 1885; May 13, 20, June 3, September 2, 1886.

South Haven New Era: May 29, August 14, 1886.

Wichita Eagle: December 27, 1887.

Wichita Daily Beacon: October 21, 1898.

A History of Railroad Construction and Abandonment within the State of Kansas, December 1995 update, Kansas Corporation Commission.

First Growth Plan:

Ghost Railroads of Kansas, by Robert Collins; South Platte Press, 1997.

Kansas: The History of the Sunflower State, 1854-2000, by Craig Miner; University Press of Kansas, 2002.

Railroads of Lawrence, Kansas, by I. E. Quastler; Coronado Press, 1979.

"The Railroad Convention of 1860, "by George W. Glick; **Kansas Historical Collections**, Volume 9, 1906.

Daily Times (Leavenworth): October 19, 20, 21, 1860.

Emporia News: October 20, 1860.

Freedom's Champion (Atchison): October 27, 1860.

Lawrence Republican: October 18, 25, November 8, 1860.

Neosho Valley Register (Burlington): October 24, 1860.

Kansas State Record (Topeka): October 20, 27, November 3, 10, 1860.

Western Kansas Express (Manhattan): October 20, 1860.

Wyandotte Commercial Gazette: October 20, 27, November 3, 1860.

Frisco's Halstead Branch:

Frisco Folks: Stories of the steam days on the Frisco Road, by William E. Bain; Sage Books, Denver, 1961.

Ghost Railroads of Kansas, by Robert Collins; South Platte Press, 1997.

The St. Louis – San Francisco Transcontinental Railroad, The Thirty-Fifth Parallel Project, by H. Craig Miner; University Press of Kansas, 1972.

Halstead Herald: January 13, 1887; July 19, 1888.

Halstead Independent: May 20, 27, October 14, 21, November 11, 18, December 2, 9, 16, 1881; January 6, 13, 20, 27, February 24, April 7, 1882; August 2, September 13, 20, 27, October 18, November 15, 1889.

Wichita Beacon: May 5, 1888; September 14, 1889.

Wichita Eagle: September 16, 1880; March 17, November 3, 1881; November 25, 1885; September 12, 1889.

ABOUT THE AUTHOR

Robert Collins is the author of numerous nonfiction works. His book, **Jim Lane: Scoundrel, Statesman, Kansan**, published in 2007 by Pelican, was a finalist for biography of the year as voted by the Society of Midland Authors. Pelican released his biography of a Kansas Civil War general in 2005. He has had six railroad books published by South Platte Press, including **Kansas Railroad Attractions** and **Ghost Railroads of Kansas**. He self-published his seventh railroad book, **The Race to Indian Territory**, in 2005. He has sold dozens of artcles to periodicals such as *Working Writer*; *Wild West*; *Chronicle of the Old West*; and *Territorial Magazine.*

Mr. Collins is also the author of the science-fiction novel **Expert Assistance**, published by Asylett Press in 2007. He has sold over 70 short science-fiction and fantasy stories to magazines such as *Marion Zimmer Bradley's Fantasy Magazine*; *Tales of the Talisman*; *Space Westerns*; *The Fifth Di...*; and *Sorcerous Signals.*

Mr. Collins lives in Andover, Kansas, and is a member of the Kansas Center for the Book, the Society of Midland Authors, and the Butler County Historical Society.